D1239756

# THE **PICKLED PRIEST**
# AND THE **PERISHING PARISH**

*Boomer Pastors Bouncing Back*

## HAL WEST

CROSSBOOKS
PUBLISHING

CrossBooks™
A Division of LifeWay
1663 Liberty Drive
Bloomington, IN 47403
www.crossbooks.com
Phone: 1-866-879-0502

©2011 Hal West. All rights reserved.

No part of this book may be reproduced, stored in a retrieval system, or
transmitted by any means without the written permission of the author.

First published by CrossBooks 06/23/2011

ISBN: 978-1-6150-7915-5 (sc)
ISBN: 978-1-6150-7928-5 (hc)

Scripture taken from the Holy Bible, New International Version®. Copyright © 1973,
1978, 1984 Biblica. Used by permission of Zondervan. All rights reserved.

Printed in the United States of America

This book is printed on acid-free paper.

Any people depicted in stock imagery provided by Thinkstock are models,
and such images are being used for illustrative purposes only.

Certain stock imagery © Thinkstock.

Because of the dynamic nature of the Internet, any web addresses or links contained in
this book may have changed since publication and may no longer be valid. The views
expressed in this work are solely those of the author and do not necessarily reflect the
views of the publisher, and the publisher hereby disclaims any responsibility for them.

# Contents

# INTRODUCTION

While I want to say that this book is not about me, I confess that it is somewhat autobiographical. In a way, however, it is the story of many pastors who are still serving the Lord through the local church after thirty years or more in the trenches. We are baby boomers, a unique brand of pastors who are faced with an admittedly surprising and serious challenge at a crucial juncture in our personal lives and a critical moment in church history—particularly American church history.

Baby-boomer pastors comprise the largest percentage of those who are senior pastors in today's church. By and large, the churches we serve are the more established, traditional churches. We are traditionalists, although many of us would like to think we're not. We're traditionalist because it's the way we think, the way we see ourselves and our world. It's the way we understand church and perceive the prevailing culture of our day. The fact is, we are pickled priests serving pickled people in perishing parishes.

I've got a lot of explaining to do, don't I? Let me give it a go. First: the term *priest*. As a Baptist pastor, it is not a term I have heretofore made too much of a connection with. People call me *Pastor* or *Preacher* but never *Priest*. I have used this term as a part of my theme throughout the book. It is a biblical term rooted in Christian history that has a lot of useful connotations and concepts. To my fellow Baptist brethren and others, I say, "Don't growl at me. Give me a chance to develop this thought with you."

Second: the term *parish*. Again, this is not a widely used Protestant concept. And we call our people *members* instead of *parishioners*. That too is significant as I develop this story.

Third: the term *pickled*. This is neither a biblical term nor a theological idea. It's a word I chose because it is descriptive of a spiritual condition that has a powerful influence in our lives and ministry. In the colloquial sense, it means to be intoxicated. Let me dispel that meaning here and now. Interestingly, the disciples were accused of being drunk, or *pickled*, on the day of Pentecost, because they were filled with the Spirit. Some just didn't understand. Some still don't. The reason I use the term *pickled* is because we are shaped and molded in our worldview by the solution of various juices and spices in our lives that preserve us in a certain powerful way—like pickles! This solution consists of spiritual formation in the home and church, denominational affiliation, theological training, and personal experiences. In short, as baby boomers, we are preserved in the solution of the church culture of the twentieth century, and there's no escaping that. And that is the problem.

As for me, I'm a Southern boy—a Southern Baptist, no less. I grew up in a strong Christian family in a small town in South Carolina. I was *pickled* early in life, as I will explain in this story. When God called me to join him in the gospel ministry, I became a *pickled priest*. And, like many others, I am presently serving in a traditional church in a small town, terribly frustrated in trying to figure out how I can effectively lead this wonderful church toward renewal, restoration, and vitality once again. It may have something to do with this whole *postmodern* thing. The problem is, to state it another way, that we are *modern* priests, serving in a *modern* church in a *postmodern* world, and we've lost touch with the world we have partnered with Jesus to redeem. The old bridges aren't working for us anymore. We've got to build new ones.

People are perishing in record numbers as the population surges; at the same time, the church is losing ground and losing influence in the present culture. Our churches are perishing, languishing, and disappearing. This crisis cannot be overstated, and I don't think I have. Nevertheless, the church has been at its best when the times were at their worst. We live in such a time, and I believe that we as baby-boomer pastors have a unique opportunity to make a significant contribution to the church's renewal and the new work that Jesus, the Head of the Body, has perhaps already begun.

Pickled as we are, we can change. God can transform us, and in transforming us, he will transform the church through the pruning process in which he seasonally engages, both individually and corporately—all for much fruit and for his glory and pleasure.

If you are one of those frustrated and frantic pickled priests, you're not alone. I just want to encourage you. That may be all I can do for you. I can't offer you a roadmap to revival. I can't point to a glowing record of great success. I can't suggest twelve steps to recovery for you or your church. But here's what I can do: I can remind you that you were called by God to be a priest before him, serving and ministering in his name. I can encourage you to remember that fire in your bones; and maybe this story will be something like an unexpected gust of wind that will "fan into flame the gift of God, which is in you" (2 Tim 1:6 NIV).

If nothing else, maybe you will hear someone who is where you are, say, "I understand," and that might be just the portion of grace you need today. If that is all that this story brings to your life, it's worth it.

# CHAPTER ONE

# How I Became a Pickled Priest

"I have been reminded of your sincere faith, which first
lived in your grandmother Lois and in your mother
Eunice and, I am persuaded, now lives in you also."

—2 TIMOTHY 1:5

I don't remember what prompted the idea. It seemed like a ludicrous thought, but it turned into a poem.

I was a seminary student at the time and at some point had come to the realization that I was already pretty set in my beliefs and in my understanding of my call into the ministry. I was a pickled priest.

Not unlike others, I had struggled with surrendering to that very real call of God upon my life. The Lord began to deal with me when I was a young teenager, but even then I was aware, to a degree, that the call was not something I could ignore or misinterpret. During my junior year of high school, I made an appointment to talk to my pastor. I told him about my sense of calling and that I wanted to make sure I wasn't misunderstanding what God was doing in my life. Was he calling me to a greater commitment to the Christian life, or was I hearing him call me to serve him in "full-time Christian vocation," as it is commonly referred to?

My pastor, who has always been a great source of encouragement to me even to this day, counseled with me gently and lovingly. Though not one who ever minced his words, and known for his forthrightness and candor, he gave me some words of great wisdom. He said to me, "Hal, when God places a call

1

on someone's life, he will not let him go. If this sense of call is real, it will persist and become clear to you. You will come to a point where you either surrender to that call or not. God will do his part to clarify the call as you seek him in prayer. Then you will have to answer the call or not answer the call. I can't tell you that this is what God is doing with you. But I can tell you from personal experience that if God is calling you, he will not let you go."

What I took away from that good counsel was that this sense of a call would persist or subside. It would become clarified, or it would go away. As time went by, it did not go away. To my shame, however, I pushed it away and made my own plans. I wanted to follow in my father's footsteps and go into the practice of law, and that was my goal my first three and a half years of college. I not only pushed the call away, I pushed God away and lived for myself.

Thankfully, however, my pastor was right. God didn't go away, and neither did the call. It stayed with me no matter how far from God I traveled. All along my waywardness, the call persisted and even grew stronger. As the Holy Spirit convicted me of my sinful lifestyle, prodding me to return to the Lord, He was convincing me as well that God would not let go of me. He was urging me to surrender to both the Lordship of Christ and to his call.

One of the problems I created for myself was that I had told everyone I was going to law school after graduating from college, including my fiancée. She was the daughter of a prominent lawyer in our hometown, and she was, understandably, comfortable with the promise of life with a lawyer. Elliott and I got married my senior year at the University of South Carolina. As I was finishing up my undergraduate work, I began preparations for taking the law school entrance exam. This exam is a notoriously difficult exam, unlike any exam I had taken before. I remember very vividly how—even in the midst of the complex and confusing questions, as I was trying to sort out the right answers—God was speaking to me. "You know this isn't for you. You know this isn't the life I have planned for you. You know I have something else for you to do. You know what you need to do." It was very unnerving.

I recall walking away from that exam on the way back to our apartment, thinking, *I know what I have to do.* I put the exam out of my mind and lost complete interest in the results as I began to pray and ask God to help me change course and come to terms with his call. I surrendered. For me, it was a great release. I felt a great burden lifting from my life. I was set free, even in surrender. But the challenges didn't disappear, to say the least.

I had thought it through to some extent. I had even chosen a seminary. So when I broke the news to Elliott, she cried for three days. This was not what she had imagined our life together would be like. She protested a little. She couldn't be a pastor's wife; she didn't play the piano! And she cried, "Seminary? Texas?" All she could imagine were tumbleweeds and cactus plants strewn across a dry and barren land! And she cried some more. But she also remembered the words of her godly grandmother when she was just a little girl: "You're going to marry a preacher when you grow up." *A curse!* she thought as she remembered it, and she cried some more—maybe even harder.

We talked, cried, and prayed for days. I contacted the seminary and soon got some information in the mail. It had pictures of a beautiful campus and stately buildings. There were no pictures of tumbleweeds or cactus plants. The information described campus life and opportunities in the city of Fort Worth. We began to see a good plan coming together. The clouds were beginning to disappear, and things began to look a lot brighter for us. If Elliott went to school year-round, she could finish her education degree in a year; then we could make our way to Fort Worth, where she could find a teaching position while I worked on my seminary education.

The next year, we loaded our Vega station wagon, said good-bye to family and friends, and headed off to Fort Worth, Texas, to begin a new and exciting chapter of our lives together. (By the way, Elliott still tells everyone that I tricked her into marrying me by promising her I was going to law school. I'm not quite sure she has completely forgiven me for that.) The trip to Fort Worth from our hometown by car is about twenty-three hours. We broke the trip up into two days, spending the night in Meridian, Mississippi, rolling into Fort Worth the next afternoon.

On the way, I couldn't help but remember sitting quietly with my grandmother when I was a child, listening to her own stories about Fort Worth in the early days of Southwestern Baptist Theological Seminary. I remember her describing their four-day train trip from North Carolina. I remembered how she painted a picture of my grandfather and her looking out the window at the colorful countryside hour after hour, anticipating what lay ahead in Fort Worth on Seminary Hill. She had mentioned a name that, at the time, didn't mean much to me, but I never forgot it. The name was Dr. B. H. Carroll. My grandmother spoke of him with great respect and lauded the influence this man and others had had on my grandfather in particular. All of that came back to me with great impact. I began to see how the legacy of my grandparents was being played out in my own life as Elliott and I made our way to Seminary Hill where we would be connected to a spiritual legacy that has influenced generations of Baptist preachers, missionaries, and Christian workers.

Maybe it was that sense of legacy and the strong spiritual formation of my upbringing that gave rise to the realization that I was indeed a pickled priest. I recall how many of my friends counseled me as Elliott and I prepared to go to Southwestern: "Hal, don't let them change you." Some offered their opinions of seminary education with a degree of skepticism. "Don't let those professors out there sway your beliefs, Hal. Don't let them change you." I listened, but it never occurred to me that seminary would do anything but strengthen my core beliefs. I never thought for a moment that seminary professors would change me in any way other than better preparing me for ministry.

My Southwestern experience and education were excellent. Almost without exception, every class was a positive learning experience for me, and every professor was a man of God devoted to equipping students with the best theological education. If I changed at all, it was in spiritual growth and a deepening of the core convictions of my life. The pickling process continued to play out in me rather than undoing or undermining the foundation that had been laid for me.

A year or so into my seminary experience, all this seemed clear to me. I was a pickled priest, and seminary was only adding to the process. A poem began to grow in my mind, which I jotted on some scratch paper between classes while drinking coffee and eating donuts in the seminary cafeteria. Sometimes during my studies at home, a line would come to me, and I'd add it to the others I had accumulated until it was time to bring them together as a whole.

As amateurish as it most certainly is, this is the poem I wrote:

## The Pickled Priest

*I've been in the pickle juice so long,*
*I know what I taste like.*
*I know what I look like.*
*And I'm sure I sound just like one.*
*You can tell I come from the garden*
*When you hear me say, "Oh, my Lord!"*
*In that Southern sort of way.*
*But a pickle is a pickle anyway,*
*And I'm one.*
*The juice did it. It always does.*
*And a fellow who's a pickle*
*Isn't about to be found*
*In a jar of blackberry jam.*
*And that's a shame,*
*Because a pickle and a berry, eaten, end up the same.*
*But that's the way it's been done for so long.*
*Try telling Grandma to can the cucumbers with the corn,*
*Or preserve peaches with the pickles.*
*A pickle is a pickle anyway,*
*And I'm a pickle.*
*Luther was a pickle, too.*
*Somehow, though, he jumped the jar*
*And jilted the juice*
*And got almost unpickled for the priesthood.*
*Well, a pickled priest I guess he really was.*
*And I'm one, too.*
*"Oh, gracious Gawd,*
*Make me a more perfect pickled priest."*

I love being a pickled priest. I also love pickles. There's usually a jar of them in my refrigerator. The thing about pickles is that they last forever. If a jar of them gets hidden behind a stack of leftovers and is gloriously rediscovered a few months later to go with the burgers cooked on the grill, you don't even think about an expiration date. You don't worry about them going bad after a while, because they're preserved to withstand the ravages of time that overtake and alter other foods.

Do you know the history of pickles? It's quite fascinating, really. According to *The Food Museum Online Exhibit* and the Mt. Olive Pickle Company, "The history of pickles stretches so far back into antiquity that no definite time has been established for their origin, but they are estimated to be over 4,000 years old." Cucumbers are native to India. There seems to be evidence that around 2030 BC, cucumbers were brought to the Tigris Valley where they were grown and first preserved and eaten as pickles. Depending on the version of the Bible you use, cucumbers are mentioned twice in the Bible (Num. 11:5; Isaiah 1:8, NIV).

According to the Food Museum website, some of history's most famous people were pickle enthusiasts. Here are a few interesting claims:

(1) In 850 BC Aristotle praised the healing effects of cured cucumbers.

(2) Cleopatra attributed a portion of her beauty to pickles.

(3) Julius Caesar thought pickles had an invigorating effect, so, naturally, he shared them with his legions.

(4) Christopher Columbus introduced pickles to the New World.

(5) George Washington was a pickle fan, as were John Adams and Dolly Madison.

The term *pickle* has one main definition. It is defined as "a cucumber, or some other vegetable, which has been preserved in brine or vinegar." There are a couple of other ways in which it is used. *To be in a pickle* means that one is in an awkward or difficult situation. *To be pickled* is slang for being intoxicated or drunk. Let's be clear that I'm not using the term in reference to imbibing preachers.

Sticking with the primary definition, there are many kinds of pickles. I remember as a kid often stopping by a country store with my duck-hunting buddies after a morning at the lake to get a soft drink and a honey bun. There, prominently displayed on the counter of Mr. Peagler's store, were jars of pickled things. There was a large jar of pickled eggs. Next to it was a jar of pickled pigs' feet and a jar of pickled chicken feet. I stuck with the honey bun, but this was a common sight you could find in just about any of the many country stores in rural Berkeley County at that time.

The pickling process is a very simple way of preserving things that would otherwise quickly spoil. Cucumbers (or chicken feet—cooked first, of course) are placed in a solution of vinegar, salt, and other spices. This is the pickle juice, and it's in this juice that the cucumbers are transformed over time from a fresh vegetable into a well-preserved pickle.

In the Christian life, we call this process of transformation by several names. We call it discipleship, indoctrination, and spiritual formation. That's how we all become pickles. We are a pickled people in the salty solution of spiritual formation, along with the spices of cultural context.

My spiritual formation—my *pickling*—began at birth really. My parents were both godly Christians who lived out their faith publicly and privately the same. Together they were the two biggest influences in my life. I spent my childhood on West Street in Moncks Corner, a dead-end street named for my grandfather who built the first house on this street in the 1930s. Among our neighbors were my two uncles and their families. We enjoyed a close-knit neighborhood of family and friends.

As a child, I was blessed to spend a lot of time with Papa and Nanny. I watched Papa in his workshop and Nanny in her kitchen. I was often there as Papa tended his chickens and his vegetable garden, and I "helped" Nanny make her mouthwatering homemade biscuits, which the three of us consumed after dinner with melted butter and molasses. All the while, I was being pickled by the teaching of their stories and their lives.

Papa came from Virginia. He came to Christ at an early age and surrendered to the call to ministry. He graduated from Wake Forest, a North Carolina Baptist college at the time, and began his pastoral ministry soon afterward. As a single man, he was called to become pastor of First Baptist Church, Kernersville, North Carolina. One of his deacons was a man I would later know as Grandpa Joyce. Grandpa Joyce was a storekeeper in Kernersville who had several young daughters. One of his daughters, Imel, captured the attention and affections of my grandfather. They would later marry and, soon afterward, board a train for Fort Worth.

After his seminary training, Papa served as pastor of several churches in North and South Carolina. His last pastorate was in Moncks Corner where he lived the rest of his life. His pastorate in Moncks Corner was from 1930 until 1939, during the difficult days of the Great Depression. He was one of very few Baptist Ministers during those trying years, because many of the churches could not afford to pay a preacher. My father recalls how, as a young teenager, he often drove Papa from church to church, holding services for many of the rural churches, ministering to the sick, helping the needy, and baptizing the new believers. He would routinely preach at First Baptist Church and, on a rotating basis, hold afternoon services in one church or another. Thinking about how difficult those days must have been, it's hard for me to imagine how he pulled it off. Even today, I run into elderly saints still in some of those churches, who tell me about my grandfather's ministry.

Papa had to resign his pastorate at First Baptist Church following a devastating accident. He had a tendency toward absentmindedness— apparently a trait I inherited—and one day in downtown Moncks Corner, he cranked up his Model T Ford while it was still in gear. The hand crank was at the front of the car, of course, and as he cranked the Model T it lurched forward, pinning him against a building. It crushed one of his legs so severely that his leg had to be amputated. In time he adjusted brilliantly to his handicap but resigned from his pastorate. For the rest of life, he continued to serve the Lord and the churches of Berkeley County. Before he died in 1957, when I was a child about seven years old, I remember hearing him preach at a homecoming service at one of the rural churches.

Nanny continued to be a very strong influence in my life. Living alone, she enjoyed the visits of her grandchildren. She instilled in each of us a real and lasting sense of identity in Christ. Even as a teenager, I would often just sit with her for hours. I'd comb her hair, which she loved, as she told and retold stories of her youth in Kernersville, the seminary days, life in the ministry, and the faithfulness of God.

By the time I was coming along in my childhood development, First Baptist was growing and thriving. The church had moved down Main Street to a new location and a new facility—a beautiful red-brick sanctuary with a tall, copper-covered steeple and two-story educational building. I went through every program known to Baptist churches. I was in Sunday school, Sunbeams, Training Union, and Vacation Bible School. I participated in sword drills, was active in RA's, and attended youth fellowships and yearly revival services. I was blessed with strong and able Sunday school teachers and devoted youth workers. There were many godly men in our church who mentored me and set an example for me of Christian manhood. My own dad was the chief manhood model for my life. When I was nine years old, I began to understand my need of a personal relationship with Jesus. The Holy Spirit was convicting me of my sins. I was not at peace. I couldn't ignore the Lord's strong call of salvation and the forgiveness he offered. I was a good boy, but I wasn't good enough. I needed to confess my sins and receive Jesus as my Savior. One Sunday morning, sitting on the third pew on the organ side of the sanctuary with my family, I stepped out to publicly profess my personal faith in Jesus. It was the greatest decision of my life.

As you can see, I was pickled in the juice of a joyous childhood. I was taught the Word faithfully at home and at church. I had many godly influences all around me constantly. What I didn't realize was that as good and as powerful as these positive influences were in my life, I was also being pickled in the context of the church culture of that unique period, a culture that continues to exert its hold on me and on so many others of my generation. In many ways, we are prisoners of this powerful past.

I didn't enter the ministry, however, as a result of these influences. I surrendered to the ministry because the Lord called me, and I answered the call with a very strong idea of what this calling meant and how I would spend the rest of my life. A few surprises awaited me.

"But as for you, continue in what you have learned and have become convinced of, because you know those from whom you learned it."

—2 TIMOTHY 3:14

- CHAPTER TWO -

# Prophet, Priest, and Prisoner

"For this reason I, Paul, the prisoner of Christ
Jesus for the sake of you Gentiles ..."

—EPHESIANS 3:1

When Elliott and I drove our heavily laden Vega station wagon out of Moncks Corner, South Carolina, on a hot and humid day in August of 1974, we had good reason to believe we were saying good-bye to our beloved hometown—for seminary and then, only God knew. In our minds, Moncks Corner, South Carolina, where both our families resided, would be a destination for vacations and occasional visits in the future. Pastors almost never return to their hometowns. We just accepted that and were ready to go wherever God led us.

After graduating from Southwestern in December 1977, we came back home. Elliott was six months pregnant with our first child, and I didn't have a church. I had seriously considered working on my doctorate and had not made much effort in getting my résumé out to churches or to some of the Baptist associations. Since Elliott was so far along in her pregnancy, and because most of our contacts were in South Carolina, we made the decision to pack up and move home—temporarily, we were sure. We thought it would be good to be home when our son was born, and we were right about that. We were wrong about *temporary*.

Several opportunities developed, but nothing materialized for me to pastor that first few months. As it turned out, First Baptist was in an aggressive stage of church planting. One mission had already started and needed a part-time pastor. In April of 1978, I was called as Mission Pastor, ordained, and began my ministry building a church. Just two months later, First Baptist planted another mission church in a different area and called me as Mission Pastor there as well. I had my hands full. For three years, I served as Mission Pastor of two missions. By 1981, the first mission church had grown to the point that it was ready to be organized into a full-time, self-sustaining church, and I was called as the first pastor of Berkeley Baptist Church, about five miles from First Baptist.

As we prepared the mission church for organization, there was only one way to structure the church as far, as we were concerned. We took a copy of the constitution and by-laws of First Baptist and just changed the wording to make it fit our identity. The daughter church became a smaller version of the mother church. We structured our programs and ministries in the likeness of First Baptist. How First Baptist functioned seemed successful and became our model: Sunday morning worship at 11:00 (First Baptist had two traditional worship services at the time), Sunday night services at 7:00, and Wednesday night prayer meeting. We formed a fully age-graded Sunday school program and a Sunday evening discipleship program. We established youth and children's ministries along the lines of First Baptist—and most Southern Baptist Churches for that matter: RAs (Royal Ambassadors) and GAs (Girls in Action), Brotherhood, and WMU (Women's Missionary Union). We conducted revival services at least once a year, and the church grew. We built an educational building with office space to meet our growing needs. Those early days of my ministry were truly some of the most rewarding. The Lord blessed us, and his presence was real. We were one, big, happy family. It's difficult to describe the excitement of those days. Then we hit a brick wall.

About five years into this great adventure, I noticed that this one, big, happy family had become one, big, content family. There is a subtle but significant difference. We had become satisfied right where we were and had reached a plateau. We were sitting on our laurels. We weren't hungry anymore. We weren't growing anymore. We were maintaining the status quo, and that was okay. I was, certainly, party to this mindset.

One day I realized how weary I had become. For some time I had been feeling like I had run a marathon and needed some rest. I was exhausted. I was too young to be so tired! I think we were all very tired, but nobody admitted it. I know I didn't. We had good leaders and faithful workers who had labored so hard and so willingly to build this church, and we hadn't stopped; but it had begun to feel like we were running with lead in our feet, walking in a low-country bog.

Unfortunately, I think I did a good job covering up my weakness and sense of growing weariness. I was not completely honest with the church. I was afraid of the truth. I was a prisoner trapped in success, shackled in the chains of dishonesty. I was spiritually dry and emotionally drained. The spirit was willing, but the flesh was failing me, and I was failing the Lord and the people I served as pastor.

There was another very large ingredient in this recipe that was cooking in my personal kitchen. In 1981, the same year that I became pastor at Berkeley Baptist, two other very important events took place. Our daughter Laura was born in February of that year. A week later, Philip, our first child, was diagnosed with acute lymphocytic leukemia, a common form of childhood leukemia.

This was more devastating to us than I can articulate. The stress and strain of it were at times almost unbearable. Except for the grace of God, his strengthening presence, unfailing love, and the hope of knowing his resurrection power, we would have lived in complete despair, or worse. The church family, I must say, was very understanding and supportive throughout this trauma. We were all hurting.

For three and a half years, Philip was in and out of the hospital. The ordeal of cancer treatment is grueling, even when things are going according to plan. The pain and suffering Philip endured weighed heavily on us constantly. Our prayers for his healing were unceasing. Our hope was always strong. For three up-and-down years, he remained in remission.

On his very last check-up at the end of his three-year protocol, as we anticipated a celebration with family and friends, his two oncologists, who had been so wonderful and kind, broke down and cried when they reported on his bone marrow test. Philip had relapsed. For the next six months,

Philip underwent traditional chemotherapy and an unconventional, experimental treatment of his blood.

In June of 1985, Philip suffered an overwhelming infection and was taken to a local hospital, where my cousin Joe, Philip's pediatrician, stayed with us into the early hours of the next day, ministering to Philip—and to us—until our son died. Philip was buried a few days later on Father's Day.

Leading a church takes spiritual strength, emotional stability, and physical stamina in the best of circumstances. Grief has a way of draining those reserves, and grief is a necessary process. I emphasize that it's a process because, while the death of a child is an event, working through the grief is a grinding process. It takes time to heal from such a cruel wound inflicted by this broken world.

I never struggled with my faith. I never blamed God. I never doubted my call. I did struggle with my ministry. The people I was serving were hurting too. They were grieving with us and hurting in their own brokenness—family issues, physical illnesses, financial problems, and spiritual questions. The priest in me attempted to intercede and take their problems to the Lord. I tried to console when consolation was wanting in my own life. I tried to be strong for them, so I covered up my weakness. As a church family, we all grew from this experience and learned some great truths about our faith and the promises of God. Still, I can't help but believe we would have been better served by being more honest with one another, starting with me.

Two weeks after Philip's death, I returned to the pulpit and preached the most difficult sermon of my ministry. I preached on our victory over sin and death through Christ. I told them that we had all prayed that God would heal Philip, and that he had answered our prayer. Philip *was* healed! He was no longer sick, and he was no longer in pain. There would be no more chemotherapy, no more bone marrow exams and lumbar punctures, needles, or hospital food. He wouldn't have to be isolated from others for fear of infection. He was in heaven with the Lord and those who belong to him. And Philip belonged to him.

I understand my gift set to include the primary gifts of pastoring, teaching, and preaching. My other gifts are those of encouragement and mercy. That doesn't mean those things come easy for me. It means I work harder at being the best I can be in the use of those gifts. This is how I came to understand my calling in ministry. I would be a prophet/preacher of God's Word, serving as a priest/pastor of God's people. I think I understood the call before I discovered my spiritual gifts. Discovering my spiritual gifts only affirmed my call, giving it context and clarity. Others have a different story.

The year following Philip's death with its accompanying grief, along with the invisible brick wall we had collided with as a church, proved to be a difficult period. Those areas of ministry that I loved and worked hard at became more challenging than ever. Weekly sermons and teaching preparation took more time and energy than they had previously. Hospital visitation and counseling were more of a chore than a fulfilling part of my ministry. I was giving out more than I could give. Leading the church to get over that brick wall would take more than I was able to offer, at least right then; and I didn't, or couldn't, see things changing for me any time soon. I needed a change, a sabbatical … or something. Elliott and I both needed time to heal. The church, I believed, needed new leadership to take it to the next level.

The fall of 1986, First Baptist was looking for a new Associate Pastor in Education. I expressed an interest, was considered, and was called to serve my home church alongside the pastor who had counseled me as a youth and mentored me as a young pastor. This is how I ended up back in the fold of the flock that gave me my spiritual foundation. Not that this position and the responsibilities that went with it were easy or slight, but it wasn't long before the pressures I had been stressing over eased up and the joy of ministry returned. Elliott and I were able to continue to heal and to recover some of the peace and joy that had been so depleted, investing more of ourselves in our two young children, Laura and Brian. Brian was born in 1984. He was just six months old when Philip died.

For the next three and a half years, I was able to use my teaching gift, as well as my gifts of encouragement and mercy, in building our educational and discipleship programs. Occasionally, I was given the privilege of filling the pulpit in the pastor's absence. I felt good about ministry again, but I couldn't help but wonder if I would ever have the opportunity to be the prophetic voice from the pulpit that I once believed was at the core of my calling. I always believed that if the Lord did open up that door—going back to our original presupposition that a prophet was not honored in his hometown—it would be the door of another church in another locale, not Moncks Corner.

Once again, I was wrong. When my pastor retired in 1989 after twenty-three years of remarkable service and tremendously fruitful leadership, First Baptist called me to follow him and continue his good work; and twenty years later, I'm still working hard to do just that. His shoes would be hard to fill, but the Lord faithfully reminded me that his shoes were not mine to fill. I had to wear my own. They fit better, and if I was going to be successful, I had to be comfortable in my own footwear.

Being called to pastor your home church is an awesome honor, and I certainly knew that. It was the most humbling moment of my life. Admittedly, I had my fears in the beginning, but I didn't have time to worry. There was so much to do. For the first several years, I just attempted to get more comfortable in my new shoes and get my feet on firm footing. We solidified the staff and began working on a vision going forward. It was a time of building unity and focus for our work in those beginning years. However, being true to my baby-boomer pedigree, change was coming.

We launched a building and renovation campaign that was sorely needed. We financed this million-dollar-plus project through a capital campaign, something the church had never done. We started several new ministries designed to reach people and grow the church but experienced no substantial growth. Giving was excellent, but we just couldn't seem to achieve a breakthrough. The church remained steady in attendance, and the staff and I grew restless. (Four out of the five full-time staffers were boomers.)

During that time, there was no church in the Moncks Corner area offering a contemporary style of worship. We noticed that many of the growing churches we knew about in the state were offering this type of service. Like so many churches in the last fifteen or twenty years, we decided to investigate the possibilities of offering such a service at First Baptist. It took us four years to pull the trigger on that watershed decision, but we marched bravely, if not wisely, into the worship war.

Almost ten years and a lot of pain later, we are still offering two services, one traditional and one contemporary. Through the unfolding drama, we lost one staff member and a significant chunk of our members, many of whom left en masse to form another church. Someone has said that all conflict is about power and the question of control. I subscribe to that principle. I learned a number of painful lessons in our struggle, but one of the most important lessons is that conflict uncovers hidden agendas.

For the next few years following this destructive storm, a lot of energy and effort went into keeping our ship afloat and our crew and passengers engaged in the continuing voyage. It was rough sailing for a while, but we eventually reached calmer waters. Calm waters are welcome after a storm, but soon you get restless for some wind in your sails. You're ready to move again.

The staff and I began to work with our people to understand from the Lord a new vision for the continuing journey. I led a good group of interested leaders and individuals through a visioning process on Sunday evenings for about a year. We called this visioning process *The Spectrum,* which examined in depth every aspect of our church, including its history, its identity, structure, methodologies, strengths, weaknesses, and potential. Like a prism breaks white light into its component colors, we attempted to honestly examine ourselves in the white light of God's Word. It turned out to be a colorful and beautiful experience. Through our collective rainbow, we saw promise.

Out of that process grew a new vision: Grounded, Growing, and Giving. We see ourselves as becoming a church that grounds people in a relationship with God, facilitates a discipleship lifestyle of growing in Christ-likeness, and developing believers into faithful stewards, giving of themselves to God and others. This vision has served us well and is presently beginning to show signs of progress.

Nobody told me it would be easy, but after twenty years at the helm, I have to confess that nothing had prepared me for the challenges of leadership. Thirty-seven years earlier, I had surrendered to the gospel ministry, received a very good theological education, and learned the classic style of preaching and pastoral ministry; but I could never have imagined the complexity of either leading a traditional church through change or facing the threat of opposition—especially opposition from within.

I am not a hero. I'm not looking for a pat on the back. I'm just a priest—a pickled priest. My heart is to be a prophetic voice from the pulpit or the classroom and faithfully deliver the Scripture to willing hearers. I still believe in the miracle of preaching the living Word of God. I still believe that God has called me to carefully handle it, and I spend a lot of time studying and preparing my messages. I still believe that preaching the Word is scattering the seed of truth—that it will take root in the good soil of receptive hearts, that it has the power to transform lives, and that it will in time bear fruit.

I still love preaching and teaching the amazing revelation of God to man. I still have fire in my bones and a desire to see people for whom Christ died grounded in the truth, growing in Christ, and bearing fruit for God's glory. I still have that quest for the ideal, and I believe that the church—though struggling to carry out its mission and purpose in the world—can, with God's help, be restored and renewed in our day.

I still love my priestly role in the church and make it a priority to personally minister to the many hurting and broken lives that cry out for love and encouragement. We strive at First Baptist to minister to one another through the deacon ministry and small groups, principally the Sunday school. However, the staff and I make it a priority to be involved in the individual lives of our members where we can.

I have colleagues who hand off weddings, funerals, and hospital visits to others. I understand their strategy of equipping and multiplying their ministry that way. I, of course, employ that strategy as well, but in a more limited way. It's so easy to lose touch with the people, and I think, for me at least, that is a mistake. So being a prophet and a priest takes up a large portion of my time and energy, but that's my calling as I see it.

There is a great deal of pressure on pastors today to be more than that. I'm constantly wrestling with that pressure. Some of our most successful and highly visible and vocal church leaders are calling for a new kind of leadership from pastors. Right or wrong, the emphasis is on *leadership*. We are bombarded with exhortations to be agents of change, risk-takers, courageous, innovative, and inventive. We are hearing voices calling on pastors to become entrepreneurial, apostolic, and visionary. We are urged to study successful business models for ideas and motivation. I don't reject everything I hear and read, and I like some of it. I employ a bit of it. But to tell you the truth, I'm weary of most of it. I don't think the church is in crisis today because pastors aren't the leaders they should be. I think the church is in crisis for reasons more complex than that.

The vast majority of evangelical and mainline pastors serve in churches that will never be anything resembling Willow Creek, Saddleback, or

Lakewood. We serve in little towns and hamlets across America, along countless country roads, and in rural communities, as well as in difficult inner-city neighborhoods. We have limited financial, physical, and human resources to work with, and a limited amount of time. The needs are overwhelming, and like Jesus, we weep over our Jerusalem and are moved with compassion because the people are hungry. That's the priest in us. Building a mega church isn't even on our radar screen. We're compelled by our calling to build the kingdom of God one life at a time in our parish.

Many of us know that our churches are losing ground, as powerful forces ever so slowly erase familiar faces from our midst and erode the ground around our foundations. We know that church gains are not keeping up with the population growth. We know that many churches are standing in place, declining, or dead; but none of us have any desire to preside over the funeral of our church.

We desire nothing more than the renewing presence of God and the power of the living Christ indwelling our people and transforming our communities with supernatural and wondrous works of grace. We are not fatalistically resigned to failure or defeat. We don't subscribe to the "what-will-be-will-be" mentality. We still have a vision and a hope for what can be, and that hope anchors us in both promise and reality.

I recently sat around the table with about ten local pastors of various denominations. These were pastors of town churches like First Baptist and small, rural churches. Both white and African American churches were represented. Our discussion was centered around the question: "What concerns or struggles can we pray for one another about?"

I listened as each pastor shared essentially the same concern: "My plate is full just being a pastor to my people, and we aren't growing. Pray that I can lead our people to accept the changes we need to make in order to grow." One pastor of a very small, rural congregation openly worried that when a few more of the older members died, the church would have to close. In his words, "The young families aren't coming."

We all identified with his sense of desperation, and we all applauded his resolve to stay the course and continue to be a prophet and priest in his parish.

In a sense, we are prisoners bound by the invisible bonds of our call and our parish. We are beginning to realize that we are also prisoners of our past—pickled priests and prisoners of our religious culture. Don't mistake us for martyrs. We are not martyrs, nor do we suffer from the syndrome by that name. We are not envious of one another or jealous when others are honored. We rejoice with them for the kingdom's sake. We measure our gains carefully and our losses painfully.

Yet, we rejoice in that God found us worthy to call us for such a time as this and for such a purpose eternal. And we will not surrender to any other call, be it human or satanic. The bottom line is, we are prisoners for Christ's sake. We are not free to serve any other master, or be anything else. We are prophets, priests, and prisoners for Christ, and we are not alone.

"As a prisoner for the Lord, then, I urge you to live a
life worthy of the calling you have received."

—EPHESIANS 4:1

- CHAPTER THREE -

# The Fruit of the Boom

"So Jacob was left alone, and a man
wrestled with him till daybreak."

—GENESIS 32:24

I'm one of many. I'm a boomer—an early boomer. Born in the euphoric years following the Second World War, my generation comprises the largest generation numerically in American history. There are about seventy-eight million baby boomers in the United States.

Traditionally, this unique generation is made up of those who were born between 1946 and 1964. We are now middle-aged and approaching the so-called "retirement years." However, many are still in the work force, including the ministry, and many of them are senior pastors, serving churches of all sizes and locations.

A recent study by *LifeWay Research* found that 32 percent of all Southern Baptist pastors are between the ages of fifty and fifty-nine. Sixteen percent are between the ages of sixty and sixty-nine, and 8 percent are seventy years old or older. This means that about 57 percent of all Southern Baptist pastors are over fifty years of age, with the vast majority of these being boomers. A *Lewis Center* study on the United Methodist Church clergy in 2009 reported that the average age of United Methodist clergy is fifty-three.

It stands to reason that history's largest generation would produce a large percentage of the current clergy population, as well as the overall church population in which baby boomers hold positions of leadership, authority, and influence, largely impacting the church's spiritual and financial health, well-being, and the light it generates in the community for Christ. This demographic reality cannot help but have a profound influence on the current state of the church in America and beyond.

At a time in life when many pastors should be settled and at least somewhat comfortable in their pastoral roles and responsibilities—having worked through their years of personal growth and discovery, and come to terms with their own internal struggles with theology and faith issues and the external issues of culture and conflict—many of us are feeling a weird sense of restlessness. We are anything but settled in our spirits. Like Jacob, we are wrestling with something supernatural, an angel of God, a powerful sense that there is more to ministry—to God's people, the church—than we have yet grasped or understood, much less achieved. And time is running out.

Those who have researched our generation have identified a number of characteristics that make us unique. In an article at *About.com,* Sally Kane identified at least four common baby-boomer characteristics: work-centric, independent, goal-oriented, and competitive. About being work-centric, she wrote, "Baby boomers are extremely hardworking and motivated by position, perks, and prestige. Baby boomers relish long work-weeks and define themselves by their professional accomplishments." About being goal-oriented, she observed, "With increased educational and financial opportunities than previous generations, baby boomers are achievement-oriented, dedicated, and career-focused. They welcome exciting, challenging projects and strive to make a difference."

Of course, there are many more characteristics, and a lot on record, about my illustrious generation, but perhaps there is some insight here that we can use. Without doubt, many of us are nearing that destination, that goal we have all worked for—retirement—but we lack that sense of achievement or accomplishment. Maybe we realize that the truer, deeper goal of leaving our churches in better shape than we found them isn't looking like a realistic objective. Maybe we have this unsettling feeling that we haven't made all that much of a difference or changed anything of significance insofar as we can see.

As baby boomers, we came of age during a time of enormous change. In a sense, we were affected by it more than responsible for it—at least in an intentional way, one might argue. Nevertheless, the very enormity of the boom reverberated throughout society and impacted every institution, including the church. It ushered in the heyday of the church with people filling the pews. Our own church, like countless others, built a whole new sanctuary and educational space in the classic (common) architectural style of the early '50s, with red brick, stained glass windows, and a copper-covered steeple. Interestingly, there were those at the time who voiced deep concern that the church would never need that much space. Within a year of occupying the new facilities in 1954, the church was looking for more space. The church services were packed out. The Sunday school classes were full. The church was growing almost without effort. The slogan, *Build it and they will come,* rings true when applied in that context. Unfortunately, it's not so true today.

Through the '50s and most of the '60s, churches enjoyed the fruit of the boom, and the boomers enjoyed the prosperity and pleasures of American post-war life. However, underneath the simplicity of life that most of us experienced in our childhood years boiled the magma of momentous changes that began to erupt and flow across America, changing the landscape of our lives.

Baby boomers came of age during a time of unprecedented world events, revolution, and upheaval: the Cold War, fall-out shelters, bomb drills, the Cuban Missile Crisis, the space race, Sputnik, John Glenn, the moon landing, the JFK, MLK, and RFK assassinations, race riots, Black Power, Brown vs. Board of Education, the Civil Rights Act of 1964, desegregation of public education, Elvis, the Beatles, Motown, the transistor radio, 8-track tapes, Viet Nam, conscientious objectors, the Weathermen, campus revolts and demonstrations, LSD and the drug culture, the sexual revolution, *Rebel Without a Cause*, Woodstock, the hippie movement, "flower power," "turned on and tuned out," bell-bottom jeans, long hair, streaking, the feminist movement and bra-burning, flag-burning, transcendentalism, and Jesus freaks. You can add to this list.

Notoriously, as baby boomers entered their late teens and early adulthood in the late '60s and into the '70s, we began to express our independence in more demonstrative, if not destructive, ways than any generation before, rejecting in large measure the core values of our upbringing. We fueled a cultural backlash of rebellion against all things of authority—the government, the schools, the family, and the church. Some participated to a lesser degree.

As a college student from 1969 through 1973, I confess to being a pseudo-radical. Some of us light-heartedly called ourselves "semi-hippies"—not completely sold on the idea of revolt and rejection of authority, if at all. Long hair, bell-bottom jeans, and love-beads were about the extent of our outward independence. In fact, during the campus demonstrations at the University of South Carolina in the spring of 1970, most of us were no-shows, and when rioting broke out in late spring of that year, we were angry to have to endure the tear gas that entered our dorm rooms through the ventilation system, covering ourselves with our mattresses to escape the irritation. Irritated is how most of us felt.

Although you can't lump all baby boomers together as a group of radicals and cultural revolutionists, most of us are very comfortable with change. Change does not frighten us nearly as much as it did our parents' generation. In fact, we believed it our duty and calling to bring about change in our world, and even though we are long past the age of idealism today, we haven't quite gotten over our idealistic zeal. We still have this inner quest to leave our world a better place, to work for and facilitate some significant changes in our institutional structures, to leave a solid legacy of accomplishment, and to be at peace with ourselves, believing our lives and our efforts have made a lasting difference.

Many boomers still serving in Christian ministry as priests and pastors certainly share this inner quest. We are still driven by this ideal, and hence we find ourselves coming up short and feeling somewhat unsatisfied. Why? Even as we find ourselves at this stage of our lives and ministry—in such a time of change in the culture and our ecclesiastical settings—could it be that change, which has always been our mantra and friend, has, ironically, become our enemy—our nemesis?

We see our churches in crisis. We see attendance dwindling. We see financial resources drying up, even if slowly. We see fewer and fewer young families coming into the church. Instead, we find ourselves burying the church-builders at a faster pace, and the only ones left are the people who look just like us—when they decide to show up. And we don't seem to know what to do.

At a time when answers should come easily by virtue of our age and experience, we pastors are wrestling with an angel and asking more questions than ever before. People and churches are perishing, and we're completely stumped and bewildered for lack of answers. We've tried all the gimmicks, used all the fads, read all the books, attended all the seminars; but here we are, pickled priests—priests in a pickle while the people are perishing.

Hopefully, we will not abandon the struggle or throw in the towel, for to wrestle with an angel of God is a part of our calling and a reminder that God is not through with us. He has spared us with something significant in store for us to do.

> "So Jacob called the place Peniel, saying, 'It is because I
> saw God face to face, and yet my life was spared.'"
>
> —GENESIS 32:30

## - CHAPTER FOUR -

# In a Pickle

"Then the Lord said to Moses, 'Why are you crying
out to me? Tell the Israelites to move on.'"

—EXODUS 14:15

Almost every pickled pastor I know who is leading a more or less traditional church is struggling with the challenge and difficulty of creating and sustaining any significant growth or progress. While we might still have the fire in our bones for the work the Lord has entrusted to us, we are highly frustrated with the enormous task of moving our people forward as a force that disturbs the strongholds of darkness and stirs Satan's rage.

We're in a pickle, as they say: a serious predicament. We're between a rock and a hard place. We know we can't go back, but the way going forward seems formidable. Yet we know that if we don't move on, we'll die where we are. It's not unlike the experience of Moses and the Israelites when they reached the Red Sea. Behind them, they saw the dust billowing skyward as Pharaoh's fierce army with its swift horses and chariots raced toward them. Before them was the Red Sea. There were too many people, both young and old, and too much baggage. The sea was too deep and too wide. They would never make it across. They faced what seemed to be an impossible dilemma.

As their leader, Moses not only had to figure out what to do, he also had to contend with the panic-stricken and fearful fold. To say they weren't very supportive of him at that point would be putting it mildly. "They said to Moses, 'Was it because there were no graves in Egypt that you brought us to the desert to die? What have you done to us by bringing us out of Egypt? Didn't we say to you in Egypt, leave us alone; let us serve the Egyptians? It would have been better for us to serve the Egyptians than to die in the desert!'" (Ex. 14:11–12) Talk about a tough congregation! Unappreciative and accusative, they were beating Moses like a drum, only adding to the weight of his leadership in the direst of circumstances.

How many of us as pickled priests can identify with Moses' situation and the burden of his leadership, having led our people to a point of progress only to face the reality that the enemy is catching up with us and an unexpected and formidable obstacle is before us? There is discontent, even despair within the ranks, as they blame us and scold us without mercy. Most of us have felt that sting of ingratitude and disrespect on more than one occasion, to be sure. If we aren't being led of God, it is easy to strike back and retaliate without grace. Some pastors have abandoned their people in that desert place, shaking the dust off their feet. But if we are being led by God, we keep our heads, guard our hearts, seek the Lord, and listen to his voice.

That's exactly what Moses did, and the Lord spoke. "Then the Lord said to Moses, 'Why are you crying to out to me? Tell the Israelites to move on. Raise your staff and stretch out your hand over the sea to divide the water so that the Israelites can go through the sea on dry ground" (Ex. 14:15–16). Many of us as pickled priests hear that same voice exhorting us, just as the Lord exhorted Moses: "Tell the people to move on."

And we're committed to doing that. The Lord worked his power through Moses, parting the waters and drowning the horses and their riders in the sea, delivering his people from a seemingly impossible situation. We absolutely believe he still works through his leaders today as he worked through Moses. We believe that he still wants his people to move on, to trust in him, and to see his power and glory as he overcomes every foe and, by his grace, overcomes their own fear and faithlessness.

The Lord told Moses, "I will harden the hearts of the Egyptians so that they will go in after them. And I will gain glory through Pharaoh and all his army, through his chariots and horsemen. The Egyptians will know that I am the Lord when I gain glory through Pharaoh, his chariots and horsemen" (Ex. 14:17–18). It's all about his glory, and if we as pickled priests can always remember that fact—especially now—our present dilemma will take on new meaning; we can tackle our present difficulties, no matter how impossible they may seem, with a new resolve and fresh faith.

Explaining and understanding the present pickle in which many of us find ourselves is not a simple task. I cannot claim any expertise in this except to say that I am living it. So maybe I have an expert opinion if nothing else, and that's all I offer. As I see it, the dilemma is this: Those of us who are the "fruit of the boom" serving as priests and prophets in today's church are more than likely serving in a traditional church. We are *modern* preachers in a *postmodern* world, and our churches are *modern* churches existing in a *postmodern* culture.

I think it is safe to say that the modern/postmodern debate is still unsettled. Do we or do we not live in a postmodern world? This debate might parallel the global warming debate. It's not a question of whether or not there is climate change but rather a question on the degree of climate change and its cause. The same is true in the modern/postmodern debate. It's not a question of whether or not there has been a significant cultural shift in recent years but rather a question of degree and cause. I'm not in a viable position to argue either way. I simply observe that the world has undergone a dramatic change in the last thirty-plus years I have been serving Christ in the ministry, and I have reached the conclusion that I, along with many others, are up against a seemingly impossible barrier going forward.

The church culture of that last half of the twentieth century seems to be a culture on its way out, and the enemy is nipping at our heels to complete the job. And however fervently we tell our people to move on, and however strenuously and painfully we take small steps here and there, we come face to face with a sea of red, fraught with danger, and a panicky people who aren't always understanding and kind.

At First Baptist we have struggled with our Sunday morning schedule, changing worship and Bible study hours several times over the last eight or nine years. Presently we are utilizing a flip-flop schedule of back-to-back services, one contemporary and one traditional, and two Sunday schools. It's working, but not very well. We aren't seeing much growth in the contemporary service, and our traditional service has seen a decline in attendance. We're missing something with the younger crowd, and the older crowd is suffering from natural attrition, aging, and death.

At a deacon's meeting in the fall of 2009, I felt it necessary to share an honest assessment of our church. I gave them what I called "present realities." I shared ten realities, along with a specific maxim and mission. The following is my outline:

I. Welcome to the Twenty-First Century

    A. The reality is that this is not your (earthly) father's world. The world has undergone a monumental change. Change is taking place at light speed. It has affected every segment of life: education, politics, science and technology, communications, entertainment, and the ecclesiastical. Most of us don't know what's hit us.

    B. Maxim: Change or be changed; get on board or get left; adapt or die.

    C. Mission: Adapt. Understand as much as possible the impact of our changing culture. Understand how people learn, think, and see the world, and adapt for relevancy while keeping our core values and beliefs. Adapting doesn't mean becoming like the world. It means understanding the world we live in and adapting to it in order to be relevant, to have a voice in the debate about life.

    "Past performance does not guarantee future results" is an investment disclaimer, not a principle by which we lead a church. More accurately, past performance almost guarantees future results. If what you're doing isn't working for you now, it's almost certain not to work for you in the future. If you want results different from what you're getting now, you have to change what you're doing. Adapt or die.

II. The Sun Has Set on the Heyday

    A. The reality for the church is that things are not what they used to be. The heyday of the post-war years (1950s and '60s) is over. *Heyday* refers to a time of power, popularity, and prosperity. That day for the traditional church is over. The sun has set.

    B. Maxim: All good things come to an end.

    C. Mission: Tap into God's creative power. Develop some holy imagination. Start a new day! Create a new day for the church as God grants us his wisdom and guidance.

III. We Don't Look So Marvelous, Darling

    A. The reality for the modern church is that 85–90 percent of our churches are stagnated or declining. Our own church has been in this condition for at least three decades. Present trends are that of decline.

    B. Maxim: A church can't coast forever. Past momentum cannot be sustained forever.

    C. Mission: Renew, refuel, and retool.

IV. God Is Still at Work

    A. The reality for the church is that God is still in the church business, because he's still in the business of world redemption. God has clearly designed and established the church to finish the Lord's work until he returns. God the Father is still governing the affairs of the world. Jesus the Son is still the head of the church. And God the Holy Spirit is still empowering churches on mission with him.

    B. Maxim: God's not through with the church. God's not through with *our* church.

    C. Mission: Do whatever it takes to move people to join God in his redemptive mission, whatever the cost.

V. Leading the Church is Like Navigating a Minefield

    A. The reality is that nothing is simple anymore, and decision-making is more complex than ever. There are so many variables and factors that come into play with almost every decision. There are always consequences to every decision that is made, and often those decisions cause pain and frustration for some. The church landscape is filled with landmines. They are generational, cultural, historical, philosophical, and theological.

    B. Maxim: Landmines are deadly! Avoid them when you can.

    C. Mission: Leading a church today requires honest, courageous, wise, and visionary leadership. If you don't have leaders who are honest enough to talk about the problems and challenges, you have leaders who are the problem, because they create another set of difficulties. If you don't have leaders who are courageous enough to tackle the minefield, you have leaders who are afraid to follow the Spirit's leadership. They lead by fear and self-interests rather than by faith and the interest of the kingdom. If you have leaders who aren't wise in their leadership, you have leaders who are dangerous. If you have leaders who have no clear and compelling vision from God, you have leaders who aren't seeking the Lord and have no clue where they're leading the church. The mission is to develop and foster godly leadership in the church.

VI. Most Churches Are Striving for a Misplaced Unity

    A. The reality is that most churches try to create a unity that is non-biblical. When you hear people say, "We need unity," what they are meaning is a non-biblical and unrealistic kind of unity where everyone looks the same, thinks the same, and likes the same thing, and we all just get along and avoid all conflict.

    In the twenty-first century world we live in, that's just unrealistic. Our society is too diverse. We are too multicultural. The number of people who look like us (white, middle class) is dwindling. Those who are Protestant are dwindling (51 percent in 2007). There are fewer and fewer people just like us today, and even we can't all agree on the same thing all the time!

Biblical unity is a picture of diversity that is united in purpose and mission with an unconditional love for God and one another. Biblical unity is a spiritual phenomenon where we as God's people are able to see past our differences and selfish interests to the greater good. God is no respecter of persons. That is the root of biblical unity.

B. Maxim: Unity is a myth, but a must. In order to survive in the coming years, we must dispel the myth that we can be a church unified by surface similarities and strive for the unity of the Spirit in the bond of peace. True unity is the deeper heart attitude that we have a common cause and purpose that is greater than our diverse and selfish desires.

C. Mission: Our mission should be to strive to become one in Christ, unified around the reason we exist—to complete the work Christ left us here to do.

VII. We All Holler about the Shrinking Dollar

A. The reality is that as the church stagnates and declines, the revenue and resources to maintain even the status quo is never enough. This is especially true in the present economy. More and more churches are being forced to learn to do more with less, and this is fine to a point. But at some point you reach a position where you just don't have the financial resources to do the things you need to do to turn things around.

B. Maxim: Love makes the world go round, but money greases the axels.

C. Mission: Our mission is to reach people for Christ and develop them into Christ-followers and givers. Money follows mission when people follow Christ.

VIII. Build It and They Won't Come

    A. The reality is that facilities are important in the twenty-first century, but they're not the most important thing. People today are looking for facilities that are attractive, well kept, clean, and easily accessible. But buildings don't grow churches today.

    B. Maxim: People don't just *go to church* anymore. The church must go to the people.

    C. Mission: Our mission is *the* mission: "Go and make disciples of all people."

IX. Honesty Is Still the Best Policy

    A. The reality for the church today is that many churches are stagnated or declining, and nobody in those churches wants to talk about it. Leaders are afraid to talk about it for fear of being blamed. Some don't want to talk about it because they know it means change. Others don't talk about it because they are oblivious to it.

    B. Maxim: If you don't talk about the problem, it's still there. Hiding your head in the sand is a coping mechanism, not a solution to a problem. If you don't get a grip on the realities, the realities will get a grip on you. Not talking about a problem is a dangerous form of dishonesty. Truth is liberating.

    C. Mission: Our mission must be to get a grip on the realities so that we can be free to take action.

X. Good Is Not Good Enough Anymore

    A. The reality for the church is that we can't afford to settle for "okay." Nobody gets excited about okay. Okay usually means mediocrity, and mediocrity is often a by-product of strengths and weaknesses off-setting one another. Sometimes strengths mask weaknesses, and sometimes weaknesses mask strengths. In either case, there is no real cause for celebration, enthusiasm, and passion. We become complacent and apathetic, apathy infects spirit, and we settle for okay.

B. Maxim: When everything seems okay, everything is not okay.

C. Mission: It is imperative that we maximize our strengths and minimize our weaknesses so that we can strive for excellence in everything the Lord leads us to do.

I must say that overall the deacons received that discourse with a seeming appreciation in spite of their natural discomfort with the blunt truth. Heads nodded in agreement. I could see those proverbial light bulbs turning on. There have been further meaningful discussions over the last several months, and with each discussion we seem to be moving closer to agreeing that it's time we as a people move on.

In a recent meeting, our deacon chairman—a soft-spoken, quiet man who is a retired US Forest Service ranger—probably stated the situation better than any of the things I had said. He talked about how in the Forest Service they would often drive their four-wheel-drive trucks through the forest where there were no roads. He said, "Every now and then we'd run up on a stump, and even with a four-wheel drive, we'd just be spinning our wheels, and we'd need some help getting off. Well, the way I see our church, we're just spinning our wheels, and we need to get ourselves off this stump!" That was a turning point among our deacons and in our church.

When you're in a pickle, it's always an opportunity to hear God's voice and see the waters divide.

"Then Moses stretched out his hand over the sea, and all that night the Lord drove the sea back with a strong east wind and turned it into dry land. The waters were divided."

—EXODUS 14:21

# CHAPTER FIVE

# A View from a Jar

*"Where there is no vision, the people perish."*

—PROVERBS 29:18

I vividly remember when I discovered that I had impaired vision. It was the day Elliott and I drove into Fort Worth, Texas, on I-20, looking for a particular exit. The traffic was extremely heavy and fast. Coming from Moncks Corner, we weren't quite used to driving in big-city traffic on a major freeway. Automobiles and eighteen-wheelers were zipping past us like we were standing still. I was driving as fast as our little Vega's small engine could go, just to survive!

My eyeballs seemed to be out on stems, crablike, trying to get the lettering on those big freeway signs to come into focus. I kept nervously asking Elliott, "What does that sign say? Is that the exit?" After a while she asked incredulously, "Can't you read those signs?" The truth was, I couldn't, not until I was almost under them, too late to make an exit. It was then that I realized I had a vision problem. Okay, I'm a little slow in recognizing my own flaws!

When you know your way around a city like Columbia or Charleston, directional signs are not an issue. When you've been there before, getting there again is second nature. It's when you get into unknown territory that vision and the ability to see the signs become imperative. As soon as we got settled in Fort Worth, I made an appointment with an optometrist and discovered I was nearsighted. Soon I was sporting a new pair of glasses. I recall my amazement at what I saw. The whole world seemed new to me. I could see detail at a distance. I could see faces from afar. Being able to see expanded my horizon. It gave me confidence on the freeway, not to mention the relief it gave Elliott when I was behind the wheel. Being able to see clearly certainly made me a better driver. And it made Elliott a better passenger!

Two things have become very obvious to me in recent years: (1) Most of us older pastors are navigating in unknown territory. (2) We're having a difficult time reading the directional signs.

As pickled priests, many of us look at the landscape of our present parish and see little that is familiar to us. We find ourselves in a strange place and in a strange time. Maybe it happens slowly, but one day it dawns on us that this isn't the world we thought we knew. Maybe it happens suddenly, like waking up in a strange bed while on an out-of-town trip, not knowing where we are, looking around the room at unfamiliar furnishings and surroundings until we rid our minds of the sleepy fog and remember: "Oh, I'm in Nashville. Now I remember. I'm just visiting this place!"

We are in a strange place and in a strange time because the world we grew up in and the parish we once knew have almost disappeared. It could conceivably be the plot of a science fiction movie, but the reality is that this phenomenon is not a fantasy. It's all too real, and we have to honestly admit that we don't know our way around any more. Familiar landmarks are missing. The pace of life has become freeway-like. The rhythm of life is uncomfortably chaotic and less predictable. The people speak in a language we do not understand. When we speak to them, they look at us with confused suspicion as if to ask, "What planet did you come from?"

We come from the same planet, but maybe a different century. Speaking more to the church, and by implication to pastors, David Olson says the church needs to discover which century it is living in. "Many churches in America are living in the wrong century. Some of them might have had spectacular ministries if they were operating in the 1910s or 1950s. Other churches act as if they are still living in the 1980s or 1990s. All the churches are trapped in the last century.

"Unfortunately, the twenty-first century has arrived. A tipping point occurred at the millennial shift, which altered the relationship between

American culture and the church, forever changing how the two will relate to each other. This change was in the making for decades. After the turn of the century, America passed the middle point or fulcrum of the transition, forcing us into this new world" (David Olson, *The American Church in Crisis*, p. 162).

Adjusting to this new world is a huge undertaking for us, and if it's not easy for us, it's even more difficult for our parishioners. The longer it takes for us to adjust, the longer it will take our churches to adjust and become engaged with the culture and relevant to this new world in which we live. Failure to adjust likely means a perishing parish, even if it's a slow death. Adapt or die. We cannot accept this as a viable option.

I have come to believe that we as the fruit of the boom have been given not only a huge challenge but also an enormous responsibility we should see as a God-given opportunity. There have been hinge moments in history, pivotal periods of transition in the church. This seems to be one of those times. It will take hindsight to fully evaluate and appreciate this unique period in which we live. It's almost impossible to understand it or appreciate it while you're in the midst of it, which I believe we are. But we don't have to fully understand it to realize and appreciate that this is a big moment.

It's like getting married. You know it's big, but it takes a little hindsight, a little distance down the road of matrimony to fully appreciate how life-changing marriage can be. This is a time of monumental change for the church, a time of significant transition, and we as the fruit of the boom are in the unique position of leading our churches in this transition.

As noted earlier, baby-boomer clergy comprise the largest percentage of church leaders today. We have the advantage of experience and the leverage of longevity. We have learned a few things about life and leadership along the way, and we have the scars to remind us of those hard-learned lessons. We have a track record that hopefully gives us a degree of credibility among our people. Our ministry spans from the 1970s to the present, from the twentieth to the twenty-first century. And we have a few more years yet to give. It seems to me that God has placed in our hands the opportunity to lead our churches at such a time as this to become churches that are prepared and poised to impact lives with the timeless message of the gospel of Christ in this new world.

For me, the most difficult challenge is vision, being able to see what God would have me see so that I can be an effective leader for the people God has called me to lead. But I have a vision problem. I am, after all, a pickled priest, and I've learned to see the world from a jar. My jar is the church culture of the twentieth century. I still live in that environment. What I'm coming to realize is that the glass lens through which I see the world gives me an erroneous picture. The juice has so penetrated my life that my sight is seriously biased and compromised. In addition, the specks of spices, which flavor my life, obscure my vision of reality.

You see from a jar as well. I see the world through Baptist eyes. You may see the world through Methodist eyes. I see the world through small-town eyes. You may see the world through big-city eyes. I see the world through a ninety-year-old, mid-size church. You may see the world through a ten-year-old, small church. There are all kinds of spices in our jars that affect our vision. We are programmed a certain way to think and perceive. We all have specks in our eyes! What we need, of course, is some corrected vision—a God-given ability to see the world, our ministries, our parish, and our mission field as God sees them.

If there was ever a hinge moment in history, of course, it was the incarnation of Jesus and the revelation of God that he brought to this world. There were pickled priests in his day who were programmed to see the world a certain way. Jesus just didn't fit their perception of God, and they were unable, therefore, to receive his revelation in Christ. They largely failed as leaders to prepare God's people for this transitional moment in history. They ignored John the Baptist's plea as the voice in the wilderness: "Prepare the way of the Lord, make straight paths for him." They were too close-minded and vision-impaired to recognize Jesus as the Son of God.

When Jesus healed the man who was blind from birth, it caused quite a stir among the Pharisees. They investigated the incident, not with an open mind to learn the truth, but with a bias to condemn and convict Jesus as an imposter. In their hearing he said, "For judgment I have come into this world, so that the blind will see and those who see will become blind" (John 9:39). The Pharisees reacted with indignation at what Jesus was implying. "What? Are we blind too?" they asked him. His reply was candor coupled with a proverbial prick. "If you were blind, you would not be guilty of sin; but now that you claim you can see, your guilt remains" (John 9:41). The candor was, "Yes, you're blind." The proverbial prick was, "You're too full of pride to see how blind you are."

Later on, Jesus was even more candid in his charge of blindness. In the "seven woes" to the Pharisees in Matthew 23, Jesus labels them as "blind guides," "blind fools," and "blind men." One of the tragedies of their spiritual blindness was the effect their impaired vision had on others. They were leaders who were blindly leading others to reject the revelation of God in Christ. In a moment of divine realism, Jesus said of the Pharisees, "Leave them; they are blind guides. If a blind man leads a blind man, both will fall into a pit" (Matt. 15:14).

I think it's important to note that Jesus didn't fault them for being pickled. He found fault with their pride. They were arrogant in the worst sort of way. They were religiously arrogant. They were proud of their position, their prominence, and their power. They were self-promoters who took offense at Jesus' truth-telling and revelation of grace. They lived for the Law, which Jesus said condemned them. They were blind to the revelation of grace and truth in Jesus. So instead of humbly receiving Jesus, they opposed Jesus and were a party to his death. I believe their pride prevented them from seeing the embodied truth of God in his Son and from being party to the new work that God was doing in the world.

We have a choice in these pivotal days to be prideful, blind Pharisees—defending our turf and preserving a culture that is no longer relevant or effective in carrying out God's continuing revelation in Christ—or to humbly accept a new challenge to lead our people on a mission for God and with God. We can dig in our heels and hunker down and hide behind the walls of religious tradition, or we can humbly yield ourselves to the God who will give us a new vision and a new way forward.

All this is a challenge to the character we possess and the priests we have become. Peter says this about character and how it relates to godly vision: "For this very reason, make every effort to add to your faith goodness; and to goodness, knowledge; and to knowledge, self-control; and to self-control, perseverance; and to perseverance, godliness; and to godliness, brotherly kindness; and to brotherly kindness, love. For if you possess these qualities in increasing measure, they will keep you from being ineffective and unproductive in your knowledge of our Lord Jesus Christ. But if anyone does not have them, he is nearsighted and blind, and has forgotten that he has been cleansed from his past sins" (2 Peter 1:5–9).

The ingredients of successful leadership in these days are no different from any other day. The ingredients for effective and productive leadership consist of Christlike character, and it is this character on the increase that creates increasingly better vision and overcomes the blur of the jar and the obstruction of the spicy specks of our experience. Character trumps tradition, and vision triumphs turf.

To see as God sees means to see reality and truth. It means to see the world as it is and what God is doing to redeem it. As pastors, it means we see the church in honest terms, where it is floundering or flourishing, the way God is leading it, and what it has to do to get there. Vision is not just a vague desire for a bright future. Vision is an overarching view of present conditions and future potential.

A church cannot have a viable vision for the future without a proper assessment of its current condition. It is no more than wishful thinking to cast a vision for success without first understanding and addressing its present problems. It would be like so many who vow not to sin tomorrow without first confessing their sins today. We have to deal with today's problems if we want to see progress tomorrow. That's why so many church visions have wrought so little change. Most of them have been cast, published, and sold like fresh paint on rotten wood.

As pastors, it is imperative that we deal with the rotten wood. There is a lot of dead wood in our churches, and by dead wood I don't mean people. I mean there are dead programs, dead policies, dead methods, and dead strategies that probably served a purpose in another day and time but are no longer doing anything to grow the church, grow Christians, or grow the kingdom. Nothing grows from that which is dead, yet we keep feeding these fruitless limbs of the body enormous amounts of time, energy, and financial resources, starving other limbs and staving off new ideas from ever being birthed.

This point is stressed in the work done by Thom Rainer and Eric Geiger in the book, *Simple Church*. These authors understand visionary leadership in terms of a leader's focus on the process of discipleship, moving

Christ's followers from spiritual infancy to spiritual maturity. They rightly identify one important hindrance to this process: church clutter. That's another way of identifying the dead wood. God-given vision will be so focused that the clutter is eliminated.

Admittedly this is easier said than done. "Many churches are littered with clutter. Floundering programs and ministries are stored and piled on top of one another. It is hard for people to make their way through the process of spiritual formation because of the distracting clutter. While elimination is not neurologically challenging for churches, it is interpersonally and historically challenging. People and history are involved. People lead these programs, and these programs have a history. Church leaders who desire to eliminate programs will inevitably offend the past or some individual" (Rainer and Geiger, *Simple Church,* pp. 204–205).

What we're talking about is some healthy pruning. Gardeners are good with this; church leaders are not. God is the Master Gardener; we struggle to get it done. We are reluctant to prune away the dead wood because someone is almost always offended. Pruning is a painful but necessary exercise in the health and productivity of the individual Christian and the individual body of Christ.

Jesus said, "I am the true vine, and my Father is the gardener. He cuts off every branch in me that bears no fruit, while every branch that does bear fruit he prunes so that it will be even more fruitful" (John 15:1–2). The Gardener has no use for dead wood. He cuts it off, eliminates it. And branches that are producing "suffer" the pain of being pruned, but the result is more fruit, which glorifies him.

The strange thing about cutting away the dead wood is that one would think that there would be no pain at all. How can deadness feel pain? And how can something that no longer exists produce any feeling whatsoever? But anyone who has been a part of the pruning process in the church knows all too well that the pain is there, and it's real. It reminds me of the Phantom Limb Syndrome. A fairly large majority of individuals who have undergone an amputation of a limb has experienced varying degrees of sensation in their amputated limb, and the majority of these sensations are painful, although the limb itself has been eliminated. They even feel the need to scratch an itch!

My grandfather lost a leg in an unfortunate accident when his Model-T Ford pinned him against a wall, crushing his leg. For several days, the doctor attempted to save his leg, but gangrene soon set in. That was in the late 1930s, and in that day and time there was little that could be done except to amputate. It was a terrible ordeal for him, but without amputation, his whole body would have become septic, and he would not have survived. The same thing is true in the body of Christ. If we don't do the right thing and eliminate the dead and dying limbs, the whole body becomes septic and is in danger of dying.

Having said that, it is imperative that we have some credible way to determine the viability of a certain program, ministry, or activity that we suspect is dead or dying wood. We have to be careful not to go whacking off limbs indiscriminately and without *due process*—to use a legal term. Fortunately, there are a number of excellent assessment tools that any church can utilize. Some are more in-depth and involved than others. An experienced pastor who has done his homework can develop his own assessment tools. One problem with this approach is objectivity on the part of the pastor. By utilizing a good assessment process from a reliable outside source, the pastor is exposed to an unbiased assessment of his own effectiveness. This is crucial.

As I write this, I'm still smarting from a survey I took just a few hours ago. Our church was given the opportunity to participate in an initiative by LifeWay Research called the *Transformational Church*. As senior pastor, I was required to fill out a pastor survey that forced me to come to grips with my own inadequacies by answering some questions about statistics related to attendance and active membership and about my own involvement in personal evangelism and community service. The next step is to get as many members as possible to fill out the member surveys. We have set aside about fifteen to twenty minutes at the end of a morning worship service to accomplish this. Others have the option of filling out the survey online.

The *Transformational Church* initiative has grown out of some groundbreaking research that began in 2008 by LifeWay Research, which formed the basis for the book *Transformational Church* by Thom Rainer, president of LifeWay, and Ed Stetzer, director of LifeWay Research. In presenting the *Transformational Church* initiative to some denominational leaders, Rainer commented, "Facts are our friends and they help us understand the current situation of the church in real terms—good, bad, and ugly. This is what our research has shown us, and we want to share this encouraging data with churches at all levels of effectiveness" (*Facts and Trends,* Spring 2010). Bruce Raley, another LifeWay executive, writes, "*Transformational Church* is not another program. It is not a one-size-fits-all strategy. It is not a formula for immediate results. *Transformational Church* is a guide to assist churches as they examine where God is working and identify the possibilities for today and the future."

The reason this initiative appeals to me is a matter of incredible timing. My staff and I had been discussing several different assessment tools and resources when this opportunity presented itself. It seemed a right fit for us and came at the right time. Further, it appealed to me because it seemed to get at the issues that we are presently struggling with as a church, specifically leading our church to become more missionally focused and energized. Hopefully, the assessment tool will reveal to us some dead wood that needs to be cut off and some marginally fruit-bearing branches that need pruning so we can begin to see our way forward.

This is how I understand vision. Vision is not as much about the future, as so many make it out to be. Any third-grader can color a pretty picture of an un-cloudy day. Sometimes, sadly, children paint a pretty picture as a dream to mask a nightmare. That's often true in the church as well. Vision doesn't come to a pastor or a group of church leaders in a boardroom or on a weekend retreat at the beach where, conveniently, there's an affordable golf course and a lot of good restaurants! And lofty words captured in a vision statement do not a vision make. Listen, I've done all that. I've come to see vision more as a verb than a noun. I see it more in the present tense than in the future tense. I've come to understand vision as seeing what God is revealing today—if you're looking, listening, learning, and living by faith.

Vision is revelation. It is God revealing his will to his people through his Word and his Spirit, and the people, through their leaders, following in the way that he opens for them to do his work in the world. Vision does not ignore the future, but the priority is today. If we take care of our obedience today, God will take care of tomorrow. Isn't that the kingdom truth that Jesus delivered in Matthew? "Seek first his kingdom and his righteousness, and all these things will be given to you as well. Therefore do not worry about tomorrow, for tomorrow will worry about itself. Each day has enough trouble of its own" (Matt. 6:33–34). I believe that as church leaders we must heed the Lord's exhortation here. Let's get today right. We've got some troubles to take care of. We've got some challenges today we need to handle. Let's be sure that we are seeking his kingdom and righteousness today. God will provide what we need today and tomorrow. We must stop leaning on our vision statement as a picture of tomorrow as a way of covering up our troubles of today.

Proverbs 29:18 is often used in a discussion about vision, and understandably so. It a great verse that has a lot of meaning for us, but I suspect that it has been misused in the sense that vision-casters use it to justify their perceived God-given picture of some future sunny day. The truth of the verse certainly justifies the necessity of vision. The King James Version, which is the most often-quoted version of this verse, says, "Where there is no vision, the people perish." I too prefer this version because it uses the word *perish,* which plays into my understanding of where many parishes are today. However, the NIV has it more accurately, I think. It says, "Where there is no revelation, the people cast off restraint." The Hebrew word for "revelation" is *chazon* and usually refers to the prophetic Word of God, words spoken by God through his chosen prophets calling his chosen people to faithfulness and obedience to a covenant or to specific action. This piece of godly wisdom speaks to the void created when leaders have no voice for God. The result is rebellion against both their leaders and God. The people "cast off restraint." They become ungovernable and cannot be reined in. There is confusion, chaos, and conflict.

The rest of the verse is often neglected. It goes on to say, "But blessed is he who keeps the law." All of this points out that vision is revelation and the Word of God is essential. It is what opens our eyes to truth. Our essential role as priests and prophets of God is rooted in the faithful proclamation and practice of the Word of God. It's faithfully and boldly proclaiming truth from which we live our lives and lead our people. The Word of God is the timeless standard by which we measure our lives and evaluate our fruitfulness. We must constantly ask, "What are we missing today? Where are we falling short? What can we do better? What can we eliminate or prune? What truth is God speaking into our lives today? What is he commanding us to do? Where is he commanding us to go?"

Vision is revelation—God's Word for God's people today. Spiritual leadership built on godly character finds its accurate sight in the authority in God's Word. It finds its voice in Scripture. It finds its wisdom in the revealing Spirit who guides men in truth (John 14:26), "searches all things, even the deep things of God" (1 Cor. 2:10), and gives his servants "the mind of Christ" (1 Cor. 2:16). It finds its direction in vision. When we as priests and prophets "preach the word," as Paul admonished Timothy, the will of God will come into focus, and it will light our way going forward as a people who walk by faith. Because the Word is what it is, it will teach us, rebuke us, correct us, and train us in righteousness.

That's the kind of vision we need today in our perishing parishes: a revelation of God that will restore order, vitality, and direction; a revelation that is not a glowing fantasy of the future, but forward calling; a revelation that calls us as God's leaders to obedience and faith, confession and repentance, courage and faith. Spiritual leadership is leadership by example.

I think of the apostle Paul when he encountered the risen Christ. His conversion involved blindness. For three days, Paul was without sight. I've wondered why. Could it be that Paul was a pickled priest who was so spiritually blinded by his religious zeal for the Law, his own biased brand of Judaism, and his own particular, prejudiced worldview that the Lord had to take his sight completely? Is that what it took for Christ to reveal himself as the Lord of heaven and to impress upon Paul the unique calling on his life to be a light to the Gentiles? If so, may what happened to Paul also happen to us. May "something like scales" fall from our eyes so that we can see all that God would have us be and do, both as leaders and as churches, to be a shining light in a world where people are still in the dark about who Jesus is and what God in love offers to all.

To have that kind of vision is to have understanding. It is to see our lives, our churches, and our world the way God sees us, to the extent that he makes that possible. This kind of understanding can only come from God. Many of us as pickled priests lack complete understanding. I do believe many of us are coming to understand some things. We are beginning to realize that our ministries are floundering and our churches are in trouble. We are beginning to realize with growing frustration our own inadequacies in finding solutions. But this has led us to unhealthy places in some respects.

Like empty addicts, we have become consumers of a commercialized Christianity where "the good stuff" is sold as panaceas of all that ails us. Books, DVDs, programs, and popular personnel are sold in the marketplace, appealing to our appetite for something, anything that will fill us with hope. Most of these products turn out to be temporary fixes that raise our expectations but lower our credibility. Why? Because nothing lasting or life-changing has really taken place. After a while people get weary of hype disguised as hope. They tire of the holy hangovers that linger for months.

Honestly, this commercialized Christianity is the church's form of get-rich-quick schemes that prey on the weak-minded, desperately needy, and naïve among us—those who lack understanding. There is nothing wrong with free-market capitalism; but buyer, beware!

Many pastors I've talked to understand the issues. They can identify the challenges of the modern church in a postmodern world, but then in the next breath they say, "But I don't have a clue what to do about it. I don't have any answers." Solutions are in short supply because there is first a shortage of understanding. We lack understanding because we have so isolated ourselves from the people of the new millennium that we have become alienated from our mission field.

We don't really understand the postmodern man or the language of the twenty-first century. We have become irrelevant to the majority of those to whom we have been sent. We have the "treasure" in clay pots, but even in a consumer-driven society, they don't want what we're selling, and we don't get that. We know we've hit a brick wall. Some of us were going so slowly that the bumper received minimal damage. Some of us were going fast enough to cause major damage. Whatever the damage, we're still at a standstill. The wall of resistance has stopped us dead in our tracks. How we go about repairing the damage and getting past the wall eludes us.

The imperative is to gain a heart of wisdom and understanding. "Wisdom is supreme; therefore get wisdom. Though it cost all you have, get understanding" (Prov. 4:7). The best way to get wisdom is to ask God for it (James 1:5). The best way to get understanding is to ask questions with a sincere heart and pure motivation. If we want to understand our current culture, it is imperative to engage the people of this culture. If we want to understand the youth culture with all its subsets, we need to talk to as many young people as possible. We need to ask questions that are not condemning or condescending, but questions that demonstrate an open heart and mind to understand.

If we want to understand the religious and spiritual beliefs and the values of people in the twenty-first century, we have to have a conversation with people. Many of them have a deep thirst for spirituality and are ready to talk about it with anyone who will listen. If we want to understand people, we have to listen to them in order to earn the right to be heard ourselves as we dialogue together. Dialogue creates understanding, and understanding is insight into the thoughts and behaviors of people.

Consider this: When have we made any effort to understand our current culture or community? When have we made a concerted effort to engage leaders in our community to ask them for their perspective on community life and the issues they face? When have we made any effort to talk to merchants and storekeepers to ask them what they see going on in our community? And what about school teachers and administrators, service organizations, and law enforcement agencies? When have we attempted to really understand our mission field?

In Mark's record of Jesus' parable of the sower, he says that the Twelve and others with him asked him for an explanation. Jesus replied, "The secret of the kingdom of God has been given to you. But to those outside, everything is said in parables so that, 'they may be ever seeing but never perceiving, and ever hearing but never understanding; otherwise they might turn and be forgiven.' Don't you understand this parable? How then will you understand any parable?" (Mark 4:11–13). Understanding is a gift to those who belong to the kingdom and seek it. The Twelve were still dull in their understanding, but things would change. Later, in the Spirit's power, they saw and perceived; they listened and understood. They had kingdom-vision that transcended their earthly biases, and this vision guided them in transforming power to bear much fruit in the multiculturalism of the ancient world.

Paul's experience in Athens, for example, is evidence of his kingdom-understanding. He didn't waltz into Athens with an air of superior knowledge. He looked around. He made note of the things he saw. He spotted a monument to an "Unknown God." He engaged the thinkers and philosophers in conversation. He gained their ear. He commented on the importance they placed on religion. "About that altar to an Unknown God, may I tell you who he is?" Understanding is something Paul employed throughout his ministry and throughout his travels around the ancient world, engaging people of all kinds of backgrounds and cultural heritage. He put it this way: "I have become all things to all men so that by all means possible I might save some" (1 Cor. 9:22).

This was his heart and calling. As he saw it, people were perishing. In the same way, if it is our heart and calling, we must see what Paul saw. People are perishing still.

> "Reflect on what I am saying, for the Lord
> will give you insight into all this."
>
> —2 TIMOTHY 2:7

- CHAPTER SIX -

# Thinking Outside the Jar

"Now we see but a poor reflection as in a mirror."

—1 CORINTHIANS 13:12

For years now, pastors and church leaders have been challenged to *think outside the box.* Like so many slogans and catchwords that have become a part of our language in the church today, the idea of *thinking outside the box* comes from the business world.

According to some sources, the concept originated in the late 1960s and early '70s with reference to the now famous "nine-dot" puzzle. More than likely, you've attempted to solve this puzzle, maybe at one of those famous denominational workshops. If you're not familiar with it, it's easy to set up. Just take out a blank sheet of paper and draw nine dots or nine small circles about an inch apart, forming a square—three columns of three dots each. Go ahead. Do it!

The challenge is simple: Link all nine dots using four straight lines, or fewer, without lifting the pen. Take all the time you need. Did you get it? Actually, there is more than one solution to the puzzle, believe it or not. If you're a conventional thinker, you're probably getting frustrated. At your age, you need to watch that blood pressure!

Actually, this puzzle is difficult to solve for conventional thinkers because they usually never imagine *thinking outside the box.* That is, they don't allow for lines to proceed to a point beyond the imagined box formed by the nine dots, although no parameters are given that preclude drawing lines beyond the box. They are limited in their own imagination or by their own presuppositions about certain boundaries. (If you still don't get it, Google it!)

Business leaders and consultants used this puzzle to demonstrate the need for creative thinking to solve business problems. As the nine-dot puzzle demonstrated in such a powerful and embarrassing way, smart people can be stumped by a simple puzzle when they limit their thinking to convention or traditional ways, thus beginning a very prominent movement within the business community to develop leaders who could *think outside the box.*

As is often the case, this concept filtered into the church context a few years later. I remember those conferences in the 1990s. I remember the nine-dot puzzle. I recall how dumb I felt when I couldn't solve it. And I remember thinking, *That's what we need in the church.* "Thinking outside the box" is still a catchphrase in the church today, probably because we've done a lot of "new" thinking, which has led to minimally new strategies and methodologies. We've done some tweaking but very little in the way of significant creativity and imagination.

Personally, the phrase, if not the concept, has worn thin with me. Not that it doesn't still have relevance, but routinely in our denominational meetings, conferences, and even in our staff meetings, someone will use the phrase with all the conviction of his heart, reminding us that we have to *think outside the box* if we have any hope of solving our problems and moving our people on. Apparently, I'm not the only one weary of the phrase. Reuters reported in an article that the number-one annoying phrase in today's office jargon is - that's right - *think outside the box.* Our annoyance with the phrase doesn't mean the concept has lost its validity.

I'd like to make a small contribution as a pickled priest to suggest that we learn to *think outside the jar.* So, if *thinking outside the box* has worn thin with you, this might help a little. The fact is, we still need to be thinking creatively. I call this tapping into God's holy creativity and divine imagination.

Back in the summer of 1922, a young daredevil named Ralph Samuelson from Lake City, Minnesota, found himself longing for some adventure. Since he loved to snow ski, and since it was summer, he asked himself a crazy question: "What if I took my snow skis and tried them out on water?" Everybody thought he was nuts, but he didn't let that deter his wild imagination and the possibilities of his dream. He convinced a friend with a boat to help him try it out. So they grabbed a rope and headed to the lake. It wasn't a resounding success, but successful enough for Samuelson to experiment with a design for skis more suitable for the water. After several adaptations and several more attempts, Samuelson developed the first water skis, and the sport of water skiing was born.

Thinking "outside the jar" is tapping into the holy creativity of God and his divine imagination. Asking the *What if* question is one way of thinking outside the jar. It's a powerful question. Some of the great advances and adventures in human history can be attributed to the *What if* question.

- At some point, early man saw lightning from the sky strike the ground and ignite some dry brush, and he asked, "What if we could learn to start a fire?"

- Later, he saw a round boulder tumble down a hill and asked, "What if we could use round stones to transport heavy things?" And the wheel was invented.

- In the 1400s, a German printer named Gutenberg asked, "What if I could figure out a way to mass-print the Bible?" And he did so with his perfected model of the printing press, making the Bible available to the masses, which greatly aided the Protestant Reformation.

- In the late 1400s, a sailor by the name of Columbus asked, "What if the earth isn't flat after all, and there is a way to reach India by sea?" And his voyage began the exploration of the new world of the Americas.

- In America, some courageous men of faith and imagination asked the risky question, "What if we declared our independence from England and formed our own sovereign nation?" And with much personal sacrifice and perseverance, and against great odds, the United States of America was born.

- In the 1700s, people like British physician Edward Jenner asked, "What if we could inoculate people with a small amount of the smallpox virus to immunize them from this deadly disease?" And they did.

- In the early 1900s, Henry Ford asked, "What if we could mass-produce the automobile at an affordable cost?" And he did, ushering in the automobile revolution.

- In the 1970s, two twenty-something young men, Steve Jobs and Steve Wazniak, asked the question, "What if we could build a computer that almost anybody could afford?" And they did; and the Apple Computer Company ushered in the personal computer revolution.

The *What if* question is a powerful question because it unleashes our God-given capacity to create, invent, and innovate new things and new ideas into the world of human life and civilization. It is a powerful and necessary question, because it is a part of our own existence to be creative. It is a fundamental dimension of being created in the image and likeness of God. God has given us the ability to think, to reason, and to ponder the possibilities, asking questions like *What if.* In a very profound sense, all our creativity is a testimony to the infinitely creative genius of God, and it is manifested in many forms—art, music, literature, industry, politics, and technology. Every manifestation of man's creativity is first and foremost a testimony to the power of God's holy creativity and divine imagination. At its best, all creation, whether God-made or man-made, glorifies God.

Think further about what God has created, and remember that in our finite minds we can hardly begin to comprehend it. Think of its vastness, complexity, beauty, and diversity. Think of its magnificent design, and you begin to realize in a limited but profound way something of the incomprehensible creativity and limitless imagination of our Creator God. And man, the crown of God's creativity, being created by him in his own image, is born with this innate ability to be inventive and with the capacity to wonder and imagine.

Think about children. Even before they learn to talk, we see their inquisitive nature and their cute explorations of discovery. And when they do learn to talk, they quickly learn to express themselves in the form of questions. In fact, there is a stage in childhood when it seems to parents that their children only know one form of sentence structure—the question! They ask question after question. Why? They do it because they are naturally inquisitive. They want to know, learn, and understand the world. It's a strange but exciting place to them. It's wonder-full.

Something unfortunate happens to many children along the way, however. They stop asking so many questions, and it's not because they have all the answers. (Although by the time they reach the teen years, some think they have all the answers.) I think as parents, educators, and institutions, we unwittingly squelch their natural inquisitiveness because we want them to conform to our ways, our ideas, and our conventional way of seeing the world. By various means and attitudes, we suppress their God-given imagination and their wonder of life and even of the divine.

So most of them stop asking questions and start living in the juice of whatever jar we want to preserve them in. (Those who don't are labeled in various ways as rebels who are not very well understood or appreciated. Hey, sort of like Jesus!) This is one reason why, as adults, we find it so difficult to think outside the jar. We have forgotten how to ask the important questions, and we've also lost the imperative of inquisitiveness and imagination.

Asking the *What if* question is almost always a dangerous question. It's risky business because, if it leads to something new and outside-the-jar, there is always the possibility of failure. It might not work. It might even be disastrous. I mentioned Edward Jenner and the smallpox vaccine. Before he experimented with this idea, there was a woman in England who asked, "What if I inoculate all six of my children with the virus?" She also had to ask, "What if this doesn't work? What if they get sick and die from the inoculation itself?" She took the risk, and it was an initial breakthrough for medicine at the time. But the truth is, our imaginations do lead to failures, disasters, and even death. Thomas Edison asked, "What if I could build an electric light bulb with a long-lasting filament?" And he did. But how many times did he fail before he found success? It was something like eighty failures before he found just the right thing to make it work. I believe that even God-ordained risks end in a series of failures, because God's purposes sometimes lie in the process as much as in the product.

There are three dimensions to the *What if* question. There is the initial *What if* question that taps into God's holy imagination. There is the *What if* question that taps into our fear of failure and asks, "What if this costs me?" And there is the necessary *What if* question that asks, "What if I don't give this a try? What is the cost of doing nothing?"

Many of us in the church never ask the first question. Many who do, however, almost always ask the second question and decide not to give something risky a try. Unfortunately, the last question is seldom arrived at, and it's unfortunate, because in God's wisdom, we must always count the cost of attempting great things for God against the cost of not attempting anything. How many of us have preached on the parable of the talents and the inadequacies of the "lazy and wicked" servant who feared failure so much that he hid his talent in the ground and, on the day of accounting, had absolutely nothing to show the master?

One of my favorite Bible personalities is Nehemiah. Nehemiah was a servant of King Cyrus, the Persian. He was his cupbearer. Nehemiah's brother came to Susa and reported to Nehemiah the disastrous conditions in Jerusalem. After seventy years, the city was still in ruins, and the people there were living hopelessly amidst the rubble. This image of ruin and hopelessness stirred something in Nehemiah. He began to pray and cry out to the Lord. He was broken by what he heard, and God stirred in Nehemiah a holy imagination. Nehemiah asked the *What if* question: "What if I go to Jerusalem and lead the people to rebuild the city?" It was a very risky question, fraught with dangers and high costs. But he must have asked the third *What if* question: "What if I don't do anything?" The answer to that question was untenable to Nehemiah, and it moved him to action.

The pickle we're in as church leaders, in some ways, is similar to Nehemiah's—if not as obvious to the eyes and as emotionally charged. Our Jerusalem, our beloved parish, is in need of serious restoration and repair. Until we reach the conclusion that doing nothing about our situation, or remaining on the same course, is untenable to us, we will continue to see our parishes in peril—or worse, perishing.

I wonder how many of us pastors really know and understand what is happening in our own parish. I wonder how many of us have undertaken a careful analysis and evaluation of our church's condition. No doubt we're aware that our churches are suffering from some kind of malady, but do we know how serious it really is? Is the church suffering merely from a stubborn case of the common cold, or is it the flu, or even one of the bad viruses? While there is some truth to the idea of analysis paralysis, I suspect that most pastors of churches in trouble suffer from evaluation devaluation. We just don't see the value in doing the diagnostics of church health. Either that, or we fear it. Men are known for that sort of mentality when it comes to their own health. Thinking outside the jar is a shot in the dark until we have a better handle on what's going on inside the jar.

It is worth noting that the first thing Nehemiah did when he reached Jerusalem was to evaluate the situation with his own eyes. "I went to Jerusalem, and after staying there three days I set out during the night with a few men. I had not told anyone what my God had put in my heart to do for Jerusalem. There were no mounts with me except the one I was riding on" (Neh. 2:11). So during that night, Nehemiah secretly went in and around the entire city of Jerusalem, inspecting the walls to see firsthand the terrible condition the city was in. Once he got a handle on the challenge the Lord had put in his heart, he cast a vision for restoring the walls. "Then I said to them, 'You see the trouble we are in: Jerusalem lies in ruins, and it's gates have been burned with fire. Come let us rebuild the wall of Jerusalem, and we will no longer be in disgrace'" (Neh. 2:17).

An honest evaluation and a clear vision for the work that needs to be done is almost always a winning strategy. It was for Nehemiah and the people of Jerusalem. "They replied, 'Let us start rebuilding.' So they began this good work" (Neh. 2:18). The interesting thing is that this was the enthusiastic response of the Jerusalem officials and citizens who had been living in those horrible conditions for years. Why hadn't they acted before then? Wasn't what Nehemiah discovered in his nighttime mission obvious to them? I think the answer to that question is "Yes" and "no." It was impossible for them not to be cognizant of the conditions in Jerusalem. Yet human nature is an intriguing phenomenon. How often do we sit amidst the rubble and ruin of our own lives and learn to live with it? After a while, we unconsciously start believing that this is the way life is supposed to be, or the best that it can be.

Do we not see the same mentality at work in our churches? Church leaders and members alike get used to the rubble of a declining parish and learn" to live with it. We unconsciously start believing that this is the way it's supposed to be, or the best that it can be. Nobody is thinking outside the jar.

In his book, *The American Church in Crisis,* David T. Olson writes, "Christian leaders tend to react to the challenges in the American church with one of three responses. First is the Chicken Little response: 'The sky is falling. The future looks bleak. Is there any hope?' The second is that of the ostrich: 'We're not doing that poorly. In fact, we are doing quite well, all things considered.' The third is that of the eagle: 'We are the church of Jesus Christ. The gates of hell will not prevail against us. We soar above the fray and do not pay any attention to mundane matters such as attendance'" (David Olson, *The American Church in Crisis,* p. 115). Olson makes the case that all three of these approaches need to be abandoned for a more honest and deliberate evaluation of the church, which includes the questions, "Why is this happening?" and "What do these observations mean?" (Olson, p. 115).

The renewal and restoration of our Jerusalems doesn't necessarily mean new leadership, but it necessarily means a new way of thinking and seeing reality on the part of those like me who are pickled priests. We shouldn't need a Nehemiah to come in and open our eyes to this reality. What our parishes need is for its leaders to lead like Nehemiah—whose heart was fertile ground for God to plant a burden for his holy name; whose faith moved him to action; whose effort at honest evaluation led to a clear vision for renewal, which he cast clearly and convincingly for the people.

Thinking outside the jar doesn't mean we all of a sudden become original thinkers and inventors of something never before attempted. That may be possible, but it's rare. Most of us as pickled priests are not wired to be original thinkers. I wonder how much time we waste in our small, book-lined studies waiting on God to give us an original thought, or an absolutely unique strategy or program that will cause the church to explode with growth. Could it be that thinking outside the jar might be more about getting a grip on reality and getting down to the hard work of restoration and renewal?

For example, after your evaluation uncovers a decline in young families attending your church, you might ask, "Why is this happening?" And what you might discover is that your church's primary strategy for reaching young families is the Sunday school program. In many traditional churches, the Sunday school program is not only the primary strategy for reaching people; it is also the exclusive strategy. While the Sunday school program has been a very successful strategy for a long time in many churches, it can no longer be the exclusive strategy in reaching new people, especially the youth and young families.

With that in mind, you might want to ask additional questions like: "What if we focused more of our energy and resources in providing ministries to young families in the community? What if we started a small-group ministry to young couples addressing marriage, parenting, and financial issues? What if we provided a MOPS (Mothers of Preschoolers) ministry? What if we provided some meaningful group activities for young men, perhaps outside the church, around such things as sports, hunting, fishing, golf, or even community improvement projects?" None of these strategies is new, but they may be "outside the jar" for your church.

Perception is reality, even if it's a false reality. For example, my perception of how somebody feels about me might be very positive. I might even conclude that the person really loves me based on how I perceive that person's outward actions and attitude toward me. That would be my reality as far as that particular individual is concerned, but it might be a false reality, because that person may absolutely despise me. He may offer me a quick smile and a hearty pat on the back, but, for whatever reason, he hates me. Nevertheless, I'm just delighted by this person's perceived friendship, because I'm operating under a false assumption.

There are so many factors and variables that skew our perception of reality and lead to false assumptions. False assumptions are dangerous, but unfortunately we make a lot of them as church leaders. Careful and deliberate observations about the church's condition will often change our perception of things. Honest evaluation will usually blow away our false assumptions. One of the difficulties we face as pickled priests is that our view of reality has been shaped by powerful factors and forces long at work in our lives, and we see the world through "a glass darkly." We live in a jar. That's why we have to be renewed in our minds—constantly seek the mind of Christ, tap into God's holy creativity and divine imagination, and not be so readily conformed to the world's pattern.

"Do not conform any longer to the pattern of this world,
but be transformed by the renewing of your mind."

—ROMANS 12:2

- CHAPTER SEVEN -

# The Lonely Pickle

"No one cares for my life."

—PSALM 142:5

The other day I went to the fridge to retrieve the ingredients I needed for a midday lunch. It was the usual—ham and cheese on rye, chips, and petite dills. For me, Mt. Olive kosher petite dills are the best pickles money can buy. I could almost make a meal of them alone.

I methodically spread the mayo and mustard on the two slices of rye, placing the ham on the mustard side and the cheese on the mayo side, and closed the deal. I grabbed a handful of chips, which I nestled next to my deli-style sandwich with all the glee of Dagwood Bumstead. To complete the meal, I uncapped the pickle jar—and looked into the frosty jar with disappointment because there, all by itself like a dead goldfish in a small aquarium, floated one lonely, green pickle. "Well," I thought, "one is better than none," but I paused momentarily with the metaphor that often depicted my ministry—the lonely pickle.

I have a strong sense that I am not alone with this metaphor of modern ministry. In my conversations with other pickled priests, along with some published research on this very subject, there can be little doubt that loneliness is a common condition among us. The unfortunate truth is that loneliness in ministry can be a very detrimental, if not debilitating, factor in the life of a pastor—including his wife and children.

In their book, *Life in a Glass House,* Cameron Lee and Jack Balswick report from their research that loneliness is one of the most serious problems clergy have to deal with. In their survey, clergy members were asked to rank certain identified problems from "1" to "11," with "1" being the most severe and "11" being the least severe. Clergy members ranked "time spent in church leaves little time for family" as the biggest problem. They ranked "inadequate financial income" as the second biggest problem. The third biggest problem was "loneliness from not having a close friend" (Lee and Balswick, *Life in a Glass House,* p. 196).

Loneliness as a factor in leadership is not just a pastoral problem. The saying "It's lonely at the top" reflects the fact that part of the nature of leadership is a sense of being all alone, a kind of loneliness. Some leaders are better equipped emotionally to deal with the lonely feelings and challenges of leadership. Some leaders seem to thrive in times of loneliness. Carl Sandburg wrote, "Shakespeare, Leonardo da Vinci, Benjamin Franklin, and Lincoln never saw a movie, heard a radio, or looked at TV. (We might add, they never heard of Facebook either.) They had a 'loneliness' and knew what to do with it. They were not afraid of being lonely, because they knew that was when the creative mood in them would work" (*Quotable Quotes,* p. 220). Sadly, other leaders, including pastors, are not so inclined to accept this loneliness and use it to their advantage.

Many of us as pickled priests, immersed in our own worlds, identify more with Albert Einstein who once said, "It is strange to be known so universally and yet be so lonely." While none of us as pastors are "universally" known like Einstein was in his day, we are widely known by people in the church and the community simply because of the position we hold as pastor of a local church. This is particularly true in rural communities and small towns where most of us serve. More people know who we are than we personally know ourselves. Every time I go to the grocery store or the hardware store, people speak to me and call me by name. Many of these people I've never met. That's a good thing in a way. It reminds me of the tremendous potential I have for touching lives for Christ, but it also reminds me that I'm identified by my position more than by personal relationships.

Loneliness is not just the problem of being alone. One can be nestled in the midst of a crowd and experience an overwhelming sense of loneliness.

Loneliness is more the emotional state of feeling that you are alone with your burdens, anxieties, cares, and personal problems. At a football game on Saturday afternoon among eighty thousand screaming fans, your sense of loneliness can be as strong as on a dark night in your private study, because those eighty thousand fanatics don't care a thing in the world about your burdens. They're in those stands to forget their own burdens, and maybe you are too.

However, I think for pastors loneliness is more than that. I think it's more than a feeling that no one cares. I think it's the feeling that no one understands what burdens your soul, weighs on your mind, and troubles your heart. There is something unique, I believe, about the heart of a priest. God instills in his servant the heart of a shepherd for his sheep, and there is a sense in which only a shepherd can understand that.

Recently, after my mother died, there were several other deaths in the church family as well. I was feeling a lot of emotional stress and strain, just trying to keep myself together, leaning on the Lord and trusting in his all-sufficient grace. But my sense of loneliness was very real. Everyone was gracious, kind, and sympathetic. During that time I had a surprise visit from a dear friend—a Catholic priest whom I have known for many years. He came in and sat down for just a few brief but powerful moments.

His first question was, "How are *you* doing?" And before I could answer that question, he said, "Look, I understand. Your mother just died, and I know you haven't even had time to grieve for her because your ministry demands that you keep on going. I know what that's like, and I just want you to know I'm praying for you." Sympathy is one thing, but empathy is another. That was empathy, and empathy was what I needed. I needed somebody to say, "I understand." And I knew he did, and that was a real gift from a dear colleague and from the Lord at an important time in my life. Loneliness may be a given in ministry, but empathy is a gift.

During the modern era, the pastor was typically placed on a pedestal. He was given a place of respect and honor. He was looked up to like a bronze statue on the state capitol grounds—a hero of sorts. He was given titles that reflected this mindset, and no one dared call him by his first name. This phenomenon is reflective of the church culture of the twentieth century, a culture where the church occupied a central role in the community and in the lives of its members, and where the pastor was accepted as a community leader.

Because he was on such a high pedestal, he had to be very careful not to make a misstep. The fall could be devastating, and it often was. In light of that, the pastor, alone at the top with the unrealistic expectations of his people and the community, had to live a kind of double life: the public life and the private life. He did everything he could to hide his personal weakness, and could never talk about his personal struggles. He had to be exemplary in every way. He had to have answers to every biblical question; he had to have a solution to every problem; and he had to know intuitively and authoritatively where to lead the church. It was a lonely life.

Today, there are only vestiges of that former church culture. I see very few pastors on pedestals. The bronze statues are broken down along with the other trappings of modernity. The strange thing is, I'm not sure how I feel about that. That was the culture in which I was pickled, and there were good things about that mindset of respect for the man and the institution, even if it put unrealistic burdens on him to live up to an image based on a false perception. This church culture perpetuated and preserved a way of life that held us all—priest and parishioner—to a higher standard than is true today. Children were taught to respect their elders, those in authority, and to respect the institution of the church. Although many in the church would like to think otherwise, in reality, little of that exists today.

So here we are as the fruit of the boom—lonely pickles! In many respects, we are reaping the whirlwind of the seeds we sowed to the wind in the 1960s and '70s. It was our generation that rebelled against institutional authority. In all our idealistic zeal, we believed we could make our world a better place. Am I alone in thinking that we not only didn't make it a better place, but we kind of messed things up as well? This isn't nostalgia talking. This is confession!

Don't get me wrong. I don't want to live on a pedestal in a public square. I don't need to be called "Reverend West." I don't want to live a double life. Neither do I want to serve a cold, rigid, dying, institutional organization. And I certainly don't want to live out the rest of my life as a lonely pickle, imprisoned in a jar, stuck in the back of a refrigerator, deserted and forgotten. But one advantage to being placed on a pedestal was that at least you knew where you stood. You had standing. Not anymore. The modern pastor in a postmodern world is not sure where he stands, and he laments the loss of standing in the community and even in the church. That sense of loss contributes greatly to his loneliness and accompanying grief.

There is, of course, more to this sense of loss than the loss of personal status. The loss of personal status is part and parcel to the loss of the church culture in the emerging postmodern world where the church itself has lost its standing. Olson makes an important point in discussing the transition we have to make from a Christian world to a post-Christian world. "For most American Christians, this is a difficult transition. Many of us grew up in the church. It was a world and a subculture in which we were comfortable. The disappearance of Christendom produces a sense of grief and loss. It is important to acknowledge that grief. However, the world has changed, and the church must move on" (David Olson, *The American Church in Crisis,* p. 163).

My take on this is simple. If church members are grieving this loss, it is probably an occasional wave of sadness, say on Sunday mornings, when they slow down long enough from their hectic lives to realize that things are not like they used to be. Pastors, on the other hand, almost never stop thinking about it. They live with it every day; the grief is acute, and the loneliness is scary. The truth is, we do need to acknowledge our grief. Otherwise, our loneliness becomes a real problem in moving on, and I don't mean moving on to another church as a solution!

When Ahab became king of Israel, he followed in the footsteps of his father, Omri, who "did evil in the eyes of the Lord and sinned more than all those before him" (1 Kings 16:25). Spiritually, it was a dark period in the history of the northern kingdom. A devoted follower of Yahweh would have thought, "It can't get any worse than it is now," but he would have been wrong. The Bible says that Ahab married a Sidonian woman and began to serve Baal. So just when things looked like they couldn't get worse, they did. The Bible goes on to say, "Ahab also made an Asherah pole and did more to provoke the Lord, the God of Israel, to anger than did all the kings of Israel before him" (1 Kings 16:33).

This was the period of Elijah's ministry. The religious climate was becoming decidedly pagan, and the culture was becoming less in tune with the covenant God established with the Israelites. Elijah, the powerful spokesman for the Lord, became a thorn in the side of Ahab and Jezebel. Following the dramatic showdown on Mt. Carmel, Elijah fled to Horeb, fearing for his life. He ended up in the desert outside of Beersheba where he prayed a revealing prayer about his mental and emotional state.

He prayed, "I have had enough, Lord. Take my life; I am no better than my ancestors" (1 Kings 19:4). It seems pretty obvious that Elijah had fallen into a deep depression. He just wanted to sleep. Eating wasn't important, but the Lord sent an angel to wake him and admonish him to eat. From there, strengthened by what the Lord provided, he traveled for another forty days until he reached Horeb. And what did he do? He went into a cave, of all places, to sleep some more. He was weary. He was even more depressed.

God spoke to Elijah in that famous "still small voice." He didn't come to Elijah in a mighty wind, earthquake, or fire. The Lord spoke to him in a "gentle whisper." That's when Elijah emerged from the cave. The Lord asked him a very simple but profound question: "What are you doing here, Elijah?" He was asking Elijah to get honest with him about where he was emotionally and spiritually.

Elijah's answer tells it all. He explained his state of being. "I have been very zealous for the Lord God Almighty. The Israelites have rejected your covenant, broken down your altars, and put your prophets to death with the sword. I am the only one left, and now they are trying to kill me too" (1 Kings 19:14). Depression has a way of distorting reality, and Elijah's view of reality was obviously distorted. Essentially, the Lord instructed Elijah to stop running and get back in the game, adding, "Yet I reserve seven thousand in Israel—all whose knees have not bowed down to Baal and all whose mouths have not kissed him" (1 Kings 19:18). Hey, Elijah. You're not alone!

David was another cave-dweller for a time. Like Elijah, he feared for his life and felt the whole world was against him. And more than that, he felt that no one was *for* him. He felt all alone and cried out to the Lord, "Look to my right and see; no one is concerned for me. I have no refuge; no one cares for my life" (Ps. 142:4). Was it true? No. But that's where he was emotionally.

Loneliness is a natural part of leadership, but when we start thinking that we're the only ones left, we have lost touch with reality. We must be wary of the Elijah Syndrome. Loneliness can easily lead to isolation; isolation can lead to alienation; and alienation can lead to desperation, a deep depression where we end up in a dark cave, emotionally crippled and spiritually defeated.

You can see this progression in Elijah's symbolic journey from the heights of Mt. Carmel to the cave in Horeb. He began to feel really alone. Look, when you're Number One on Jezebel's Most Wanted List, you have a tendency to think you're the Lone Ranger! But this heightened sense of loneliness coupled with his fear produced a need for isolation. He ran away from everybody and everything he knew. Eventually, he even separated himself from his servant. Left him to fend for himself. He just wanted to be left all alone, isolated from the world. This is when Elijah's perspective became blurred completely, and he lost touch with reality. He ended up totally alienated from his people, from his purpose, and from his most powerful ally—God. He wanted to die. That's the Elijah Syndrome.

How many priests and prophets of God today are suffering from the Elijah Syndrome? I suspect there are more than we would like to believe. In talking to my priestly peers, I sense many of them are lonely, depressed, and live in quiet, cave-like desperation. And the Lord is asking that simple profound question: "What are you doing here? You think you're all alone? You think you're the only one who has a zeal for the Lord? You're not! There are thousands "whose knees have not bowed down to Baal and all whose mouths have not kissed him."

After the unexpected and much-appreciated visit by my Catholic colleague, I received one additional surprising contact, this time from a fellow Baptist pastor. The surprising part was that he is the pastor of that breakaway church I spoke of earlier. He wrote a very heart-felt, sincere note of support that lifted my spirits. I wrote him a word of thanks, and we met a week or so later for lunch, sharing a time of fellowship and mutual encouragement. He didn't say, "I understand," but in essence, that's what he was communicating. What a powerful, positive gift empathy among pastors can be. It made me think, "What has been done for me, I can do for others." That is really the reason for this book. It's one way I can say to all those other pickled priests out there, "I understand." If Elijah had had that kind of encouragement, maybe he wouldn't have experienced that emotional breakdown in his life.

We live in a time when the religious climate is decidedly pagan, and the culture is becoming increasingly opposed to the covenant of the blood of Christ. But we are not alone. We are neither alone in our calling, nor in our zeal. Just because things could get worse, doesn't mean they have to. And if they do, we are not alone.

> "Do not be afraid; keep on speaking, do not be silent. For
> I am with you, and no one is going to attack and harm
> you, because I have many people in this city."

> —ACTS 18:9–10

# CHAPTER EIGHT

# Balancing Act: The Grind and the Gospel

"This is my gospel, for which I am suffering even to
the point of being chained like a criminal. But God's
word is not chained. Therefore I endure everything
for the sake of the elect, that they too may obtain the
salvation that is in Christ Jesus, with eternal glory."

—2 TIMOTHY 2:8–10

B alance is a good thing to have in life.

It's a good thing to have if you're a steel worker or a log roller. It's a good thing to have if you're carrying a baby in your arms, along with a diaper bag and a sack of groceries. Balance is a good thing to have if you're a gymnast or a circus performer. It's a good thing to have if you're hiking along a mountain trail that takes you precariously close to the edge of a cliff. (I get dizzy thinking about it!) Balance is a good thing to have when you're conducting a funeral service.

Let me explain that one. Minutes before walking out of my study to conduct a funeral service for a dear lady in our church, I knelt to pray. When I got up, I was seriously dizzy. The room started spinning around; faster and faster it spun. I could hardly stand. I fell into my chair and closed my eyes for a moment, but when I opened them again, the room was circulating furiously around me. I didn't know what was happening, but I knew I was in trouble; and I knew the funeral director was waiting for me to get the service started.

I got up and hugged the wall all the way to the front door. As I held onto the front door, I was able to make out the blurred image of the funeral director on the front lawn, and I called to her. When she saw that my face was greener than the front lawn, she came running. She helped me back inside the office and called 9-1-1. Moments later I was at the emergency room. My blood was tested, my heart monitored, and my head examined. I was diagnosed with vertigo. It took a week or more for the world to stop spinning and for my balance to return. It's amazing to me that when those little inner ear crystals get out of place, you have no balance—no equilibrium—and your world is out of control. (Just so you'll know, our minister of music was able to conduct the funeral service and made some impromptu remarks about the lady that seemed to save the day. The family understood, but I'm not sure my music colleague will ever let me forget it.)

Balance is a good thing to have in life. No one aspires to be known as imbalanced. We think of a balanced life as a life of priorities properly placed and things of importance given equal or proportionate weight. We respect the person who seems to have his act together. We strive to be that person whose walk through life appears to be even-keeled.

This idea of balance was ingrained in me from childhood. I was taught to keep my life in proper perspective, not to go "hog-wild" or crazy over anything, and to keep my emotions under control. I was taught not to get too "high" or too "low" about things. I learned from many teachers to keep my feet on the ground, to keep my head on straight, and to guard my heart—to live a balanced life. This was an important aspect of my pickling.

In my ministry, I've attempted to live what I was taught. I've tried to live a balanced life. In some respects, I've been fairly successful. In some respects, I've failed. Overall, I think I would have to say that my entire ministry has been a constant balancing act. Looking back, however, a lot of it has been an "act" more than a balance, as I've tried to please or placate, sometimes insincerely, those who expected certain things from me.

All of us are familiar with this idea of balance and how difficult it is to keep it. There's our relationship with the Lord and personal time in prayer, meditation, and Bible study. Most of us have families, spouses, and children who need and deserve our time and attention, not to mention our need for them. Of course, we have ministerial duties, obligations, and responsibilities. Those three are the major factors in the balancing act. Then there is community involvement and other demands on our time and energy. To get too involved in life beyond church and home might tip the scale in the wrong direction. We have to be cautious about that.

In addition, there is the time we need for ourselves—down time—time spent in relaxation or recreation: reading, jogging, riding a bike, hunting, or fishing. For me, it's sitting in a deer stand on a crisp fall afternoon or calling a big gobbler on a calm spring morning. Those things add balance to my life—a balance between life's pressures and life's pleasures. Sometimes I think that if balance weren't a big thing in my life, I'd easily turn into a bum. Seriously, I'd be in trouble.

Having said that, I must go on to confess that I'm having some second thoughts about the balanced life. What I've come to realize at this late stage of my life and ministry is that the pursuit of balance can also be the pursuit of mediocrity. Think about it. As we attempt to balance our time and energy between personal relationships at home, church and ministry responsibilities, and community involvement, we are attempting to be good at everything; and we end up not being excellent at anything. I've been a good husband; I've been a good father; I've been a good pastor; I've been a good citizen and a good hunter; but I haven't been excellent at much of anything. This isn't self-abasement. This is honesty.

The implications of this are enormous. Because I'm the spiritual leader of my home and the church, the quality of my leadership affects the quality of those two very important families, the very people I am passionate about and love most in this life. I have to admit that this weighs on me heavily as I think about it. For years I lived by the rule of balance. I am a family man, and I love my family. I love my ministry and the people I serve, and I work hard. I'm driven, but not over the top. I'm not a workaholic, and I'm neither lazy nor irresponsible. But the fact remains that I've not led either my family or my church in excellence, and it shows. It shows particularly in the church.

First Baptist is a very good church. Throughout its history, it has done some very good things. It has shown good growth; it has provided good ministries in the community; it has a good record of accomplishments and a good reputation. It's a good church, but excellence would be a rare boast if we were honest. We have some very good leaders and a good corps of volunteers, but what we lack is *excellence.*

The point I'm driving home is that excellence is not derived from balance. It is derived from passion. It's true in any of life's endeavors. Those who excel in business, politics, sports, and any number of fields are passionate about what they are doing. I've come to see balance as the enemy of excellence. I have valued balance over passion, and so has the church. If we have passion, it's a reserved passion. It's muted. It's kept in check. In our worship services you seldom hear an "amen," although we do clap more than we used to. There are a few who raise their hands in praise, but little outward emotion or passion is publicly expressed. Balance doesn't permit getting "carried away" with anything, even as we worship the God of grace and eternity.

This penchant for balance permeates our church life. For example, when it comes to evangelism, we have had some very good teaching, training, and equipping in personal evangelism through the years, but there has been little in the way of real passion for those without Christ. I see this in my own life.

It struck me recently at an area ministerial meeting of local pastors. As we shared together some of our struggles and concerns, an Episcopal colleague confessed to the fact that he knew he needed to be more personally involved in personal evangelism, but the daily grind of taking care of the flock seemed to completely consume his time and energy. "How," he asked, "do I reach out into the community with the gospel when I spend so much time taking care of the sheep?" Everyone in the room identified with his guilty lament, including me.

My wife explains to people that I'm a creature of habit. She also *complains* to me that I'm a creature of habit, predictable as the morning sunrise, though much more boring. Truthfully, there is little beauty and passion in a predictable life. The balanced life I've pursued has produced a grind-it-out existence, which I've accepted as the ordinary ministerial life—the way it's supposed to be. After all, the fruit of the boom are geared to achievement, and we have been ingrained with the notion that achievement is the product of the work ethic instilled in us by our fathers and forefathers. We are competitors at heart and believe that the way to win is to out-compete our competitors, whomever they may be. We like to think that while they're sleeping, we're working—but still striving for balance. This results in a daily grind, and a daily grind produces a predictable, weekly whirlwind.

Does the following synopsis of my daily grind and weekly whirlwind sound familiar?

## Sunday Sunrise

I love Sunday morning. I love the Lord's Day. It's the best day of the week for me. I get up early on Sunday morning to spend time preparing my heart and mind for worship. I pray. I go over my sermon notes. I visualize the service. I vocalize my message in a whisper. I pray. I think. I prepare. I usually arrive at the church before anyone else. I repeat what I've done at home. I'm ready to break bread and feed the five thousand, more or less. Well, less.

The Sunday brunch is served. I've served the best meal of spiritual meat and side dishes I know how to prepare. People eat. Some, I think, consume the meal with an appetite for what I've served up—a good, home-cooked feast. Some, I'm afraid, pick at this meal as if it were all spinach and liver. Politely they push the food around the plate but consume very little. They seem to be waiting for dessert. At invitation time, I look for a response. A few might come to the altar to pray, but most have the look of a looming Sunday afternoon nap. I'm feeling it too.

After the benediction, I walk to the front door. It's around noon, when the sun is straight up in the sky. It's not a time for shadows, but I feel like I'm standing in the twelve o'clock shadow. It's not cast by the tall steeple up above, and it is not the refuge in "the shadow of his wings" I'm talking about. I enjoy speaking to the people as they depart. I appreciate that many will stand in a line to speak to me as they leave. Some don't. We exchange warm and caring words. Some make generous and sincere comments about the service and/or the message. I feel a limited sense of gratification in those remarks. I accept them as words of encouragement.

Still, I'm standing in this twelve o'clock shadow. "The harvest is past, the summer has ended and we are not saved" (Jer. 8:20). The workings of the Spirit of God in worship are sometimes hidden. Seeds are planted and watered Sunday after Sunday. But in the twelve o'clock shadow, I wonder about the harvest, and I'm ready for my nap.

## Monday Mourning

The twelve o'clock shadow extends its dim darkness through Monday morning at the staff meeting. We gather for a time of Scripture and prayer. There is a weary feel to it. We pray for certain upcoming events or activities and program progress. We intercede for church members who are sick, in the hospital, or grieving. But the truth is, the grieving are praying for the grief-stricken. It's Monday *mourning* time at the staff meeting.

I don't think it has ever been said. We make light of our collective quietness, but our spirits are downcast. We attempt to encourage one another as we discuss what went "right" and what went "wrong" on Sunday. The sound system had problems. The Powerpoint operator went to sleep during the songs. The organ was too loud. Maybe we need to tone down the drums too. We take turns discussing and coordinating the calendar. We spend time going over some of the same unresolved issues in a certain Sunday school class. From time to time, we rejoice in new members joining the church, probably right after somebody mentioned that another family has been visiting another church.

I don't dread our staff meeting. We get things done. We do have some light-hearted moments. We're close enough to poke fun at each other. Nobody gets his feelings hurt. It's not all gloom and doom. We laugh a lot, usually at someone's expense. When everyone has had his say, we're ready to adjourn. (Monday is my hospital visitation day.)

But there's something that hasn't been said. Something like, "Hey, I'm grieving. I'm grieving this sense of loss. I'm crying inside, because we've lost something. I don't know exactly what it is, but it hurts, and I'm sad." Nobody wants to acknowledge his grief, maybe because he doesn't know why he's grieving or how to articulate his grief. Maybe, like a lot of people, we just don't want to go there, because to acknowledge grief is to acknowledge loss. Then it becomes more real, and when grief becomes more real, you have to deal with it. Some choose not to. That's Monday mourning.

Monday afternoon, with the staff meeting behind me, I'm ready to hit the road to the hospitals. I look forward to it in a strange way. The hospitals are in Charleston. I drive. I think. I relax. I pick up a newspaper and stop into Subway for a tuna sub. I catch up on all the daily news, check the sports page to read the latest on the Gamecocks, and glance at the obituaries. I'm not mentioned! I'm relaxed, refreshed, and ready to see the sick and pray with the patients.

This is ministry in the raw to me. This is real stuff, real life, and there's an empowering, affirming feeling as I walk into ICU to see a church member who's just had heart by-pass surgery. He can't speak. He's hardly aware I'm there. But he smiles around the tube down his throat. I take his IV-strapped hand, and I pray. We open our tear-filled eyes. We feel the presence of God. Driving home, I pray. I think, and I feel less grief and more joy. Strange.

## The Tuesday Treadmill

Tuesday morning, I hit the ground running. Usually, I've already outlined my sermon, and Tuesday is the day I set aside to do the bulk of my sermon preparation. I tell the secretary to hold my calls unless it's an emergency. Back in the pastor's study with a fresh cup of coffee, I'm focused. I'm into the Scripture: studying, thinking, writing, rewriting. An important point comes to mind. I'm trying to put it down before I lose it.

The phone buzzes. "I hate to interrupt you. I know you're studying, but Mr. Blank just dropped by to see you and asked if you had just a minute."

"Okay," I say. Mr. Blank comes in and has a seat.

"I know you're busy, Pastor, but I won't take but a minute."

"No problem," I say. "Take your time."

He takes me literally. About forty-five minutes later, he says, "Well, I just wanted to drop by for a minute and tell you about this." About an hour later, I close the door behind him and try to get back to work. I look at my watch. Lunch time already?

Tuesday afternoon, after I return some phone calls, I have a couple of appointments coming in. Two hours later, I'm ready to get back to that important point and put the finishing touches on the message. What was that point anyway? I can't quite get it back. I sit there trying to get my mind back in gear. I'm getting sluggish. I'm tired.

There's another buzz. "Pastor, we just got word that Mrs. Lovely died unexpectedly. The family wants you to come over and talk about the arrangements." I close my Bible, lay my material aside, and "save" the unfinished sermon. I say a brief prayer for the family and head over to the Lovely home.

By the time I get home, I'm emotionally and physically exhausted. I literally feel like I've been on a treadmill all day long. About the time I'm ready to plop down and close my eyes, Elliott says, "Go change. We need to walk." She's right. I need to walk. Walking has helped me immensely with my type 2 diabetes and high blood pressure. I need to walk, but I don't know if I can muster the strength to even put on my walking shoes. Sometimes I do; sometimes I don't. But every time I walk that mile or so, I feel better, and I sleep better that night. Walking, jogging, or running is an effective antidote to the pace of the Tuesday Treadmill.

## The Wednesday Weakly Meetings

A lady I once worked with during my college days called Wednesday "hump day." I'd never heard that term before. I naively asked her what it meant. She said, "Well, Wednesday is like the hump in the middle of the week. When you get past Wednesday, you're over the hump, and it's all downhill from there." Makes sense to me, especially if your workweek is Monday through Friday.

I'm not so sure that "hump day" really applies to those in ministry. Our workweek is in actuality undefined. But this much is true: Wednesday is an important day, at least in some churches. Baptists, for example, have traditionally seen Wednesday night as another time of corporate worship, usually called "Prayer Meeting." Since, theoretically, members are going to be at church for this Prayer Meeting, other meetings are scheduled as well: committees, teams, choirs, and other organizational meetings.

When I get to the office on Wednesday morning, I still have Sunday morning's message to complete, plus the Wednesday night Bible Study, which follows the Prayer Meeting. By the grace of God and with a refreshed brain, I get the sermon finished and turn my thoughts to the ongoing Wednesday-night Bible study. I prepare my notes and type out the outline and discussion questions for the secretary to put on the handouts along with the prayer list.

Over the years, we've tried to deal with a troubling trend—declining attendance at Prayer Meeting. We've tried several different strategies for bucking this trend, but nothing has changed. Our weekly Prayer Meeting has become a *weakly* meeting. While it's still a "sweet hour of prayer" in some ways, it's pretty weak. I have a strong appreciation for the faithful few who come for this time of corporate prayer, but it's a stretch to call it corporate prayer when so few participate.

I'm embarrassed to admit that there are times when I feel that this meeting, and all the other Wednesday night meetings, are powerless and sometimes serve little purpose in the kingdom. The result is that Wednesday has become a "hump day" of sorts for me. I'm glad when it's over. I led the church in prayer, weak as it was. I led the church in Bible study. I've met with the committees and the teams. We've taken care of business, but little of it had anything to do with the kingdom of God; it was just business. Is it any wonder that attendance is declining on Wednesday night? I was recently told by a prominent church leader, "I don't like Wednesday night anymore. It's the same old same old."

Wednesday night I'm over the hump, and "it's all downhill" takes on a new meaning. The daily grind and the weekly whirlwind take their toll.

## Thanksgiving Thursday

I've never heard an explanation as to why Thanksgiving is always on Thursday, but I can tell you this—I always feel thankful on Thursday in a specialized sense.

Thursdays arrive with the biggest pressures behind me. The Sunday morning sermon is prepared, Wednesday night services are history, and I can spend Thursday doing some things I've put on the back burner. I do some planning, make some phone calls, and answer e-mails. I might even check Facebook. Sometimes I can do a little writing. I can do some advance sermon study. I schedule appointments for Thursday if I can. I talk to the different staff members about some project or activity. Later in the day, I try to visit some of the senior adults and shut-ins.

I'm thankful for Thursdays because, barring the occasional funeral or emergency, the treadmill seems to slow down a bit. I can start to wind down. I'm more relaxed. I'm probably easier to get along with. The staff even stops on Thursday mornings about 9:00 to have a sausage biscuit and coffee together. It feels good.

When Thursday evening arrives, I'm hopeful that I've accomplished the major items on my "To Do" list. I check them off mentally, and my mind is at ease as I begin to think about the others things I need to do in my balancing act.

## Good Friday

Friday is a good day because it's officially *my* day. It's my day off duty. It doesn't, of course, always work that way, but as a rule I get to spend Friday pursuing more personal things.

There are always projects going on at home: yard work, gardening, repairs and maintenance around the house. We might need to spend some time on the budget and paying bills. Elliott might want to go to Charleston to pick up some art supplies or shop for some things she needs. We might take in a movie or go out to eat. Occasionally, we might have some friends over, or we might cook out at somebody's house.

Friday is good because it's a balanced day. If it's turkey season, I might go listen to some gobbling as the sun rises and the woods come alive. I feel alive as well. If it's deer season, I might go sit in a deer stand. Sometimes my life partner becomes my hunting partner. I'll put her in a comfortable stand and then stealthily go to mine. I sit there in stillness as the crisp fall air settles gently on my camouflage-covered shoulders, releasing some of the pressures that had been perched there disguised as friendly burdens. And I feel a liberty. I feel as though I'm back in balance.

As evening light grows more dim and the shadows lengthen across the food plot, I hear a rifle shot. It reverberates through the timber like thunder. Elliott has done it again. I'm sure of it. She's become an excellent marksman since she started deer hunting with me. She goes with me in late fall when the colors are changing and the colder weather arrives. That's when the mosquitoes disappear. She goes with me because, as she says, "If you can't beat 'em, join 'em." That's her way of saying I've come up short on the balancing act when it comes to spending time with her. She's right, but I'm happy to have her with me—especially as we load up her deer and head to the venison processor.

## Super Saturday

In some ways, Saturday is an extension of Friday. If Friday is good, Saturday is super. I'm usually tired by Saturday night, but it's what they call a "good" tired. My mind is rested and renewed by some good, physical activity, an activity in which I can see some results. That's one reason I like to get on my riding lawn mower at home or my tractor at the hunting property. I can look back where I've been and see progress.

After the evening meal, I find myself drawn away from others and into my study. It's time to start thinking about the next morning. It's time to start concentrating on the service, the Scripture, the message, and those who will hear it. Finally, after an hour or so, tired and sleepy, I crawl into bed ... and *beeeeeeep!* "Get up! Get up! Get up!" the alarm says. "It's Sunday! Resurrection day! The Lord's Day! Get up! Rise and shine!"

Like my Episcopalian brother asked, "Where is the gospel in all this?" The grind seems to squeeze the gospel right out of the world in the weekly whirlwind that repeats itself week after week and year after year—all in the name of balance.

In a piece posted by Thom Rainer of LifeWay called "Pastors and Time," he recently wrote, "Leadership gurus will tell you that a primary skill of an effective leader is the ability to manage time for maximum productivity." He reports on a study conducted by LifeWay comparing the time management of "effective" leaders whose churches reported significant conversion growth and a similar number of pastors whose churches did not have significant conversion growth. The study found that effective leaders spend considerably more time in sermon preparation, personal evangelism, and with the family—and a lot less time performing "custodial duties."

Under the subheading "Priorities and Balance" Rainer writes, "The time allocation of effective leaders seems to complement the way they describe their own leadership style. In order to accomplish what they considered priority functions, they had to sacrifice in other areas. The leaders of effective churches spent over forty hours per week with their families and in sermon preparation time. In order to fulfill these priorities, they obviously had to let some things go. Thus the effective leaders cannot do many of the responsibilities often expected of them as pastors. They cannot make all the hospital visits. They cannot counsel everyone. And they cannot perform all of the custodial duties that may be expected of them. But as leaders they can see that those things get done."

He's probably absolutely right about that. But I suspect that many pastors reading those remarks with a twinge of remorse or disgust will mutter under his breath, "Yeah, right. Easy for you to say." Where most of us are in our ministry, that kind of so-called "effective" leadership is only a mirage, a dream never to be realized.

What we need to do is pursue passion rather than balance. Godly passion will strike a good balance in our lives and produce excellence in our endeavors. Godly passion is the love of God outpoured in our lives in the power of the Holy Spirit. Godly passion has a way of creating certain priorities that are not artificial or contrived. Paul said that it is "a more excellent way." We ought to "stir up the gift" that is in us, and unashamedly release our passionate love for the Lord and for his gospel.

We ought to be passionate in our love for our wives and children. We ought to be passionate in our love for the people we serve. We ought to be passionate for the lost and unchurched. Balance stretches us thin and wears us down. Passion puts all of life in perspective, even for pickled priests. True passion is not parceled out like a spiritual commodity in short supply. It is sustainable. True passion is lived out through the limitless supply of the indwelling Christ. It never fails.

"And now I will show you a more excellent way."

—1 CORINTHIANS 12:31

- CHAPTER NINE -

# The Perishing Parish

"He is patient with you, not wanting anyone to
perish, but everyone to come to repentance."

—2 PETER 3:9

As a Southern Baptist, I am aware that the word *priest* is not a word
we often use in conversations about Baptist work. In the same way,
the concept of a *parish* is foreign to us. The word isn't really a part of our
Baptist vocabulary. We have our own pickled dialect.

I was first exposed to the term *parish* while I was in high school and
college. My dad was a local attorney, and he employed me during the
summer months to do some title work on property cases. My job was to
search through the old county records to establish a line of ownership.
Sometimes these searches took me all the way back to the days before the
State of South Carolina was divided into counties.

From the earliest days, property in South Carolina was identified in
parishes, based on the geographical territories of the Church of England,
which was well established in the colonial period of our history. Even after the
Constitution of 1895 was adopted, these parish designations were still used
to more specifically identify the location of property within the county.

Berkeley County is home to some very significant sites and events
in American history. Along the Cooper River, from Berkeley County
to Charleston, some historic plantation homes still exist as reminders of
our unique historical past. There are also quite a few old Anglican parish

81

chapels surrounded by ancient gravestones where some of our most revered ancestors are buried—planters, merchants, politicians, even signers of the Declaration of Independence and the Constitution.

The burned ruins of one of these parish chapels—Biggin Church—stand just outside the Moncks Corner town limits. It was the site of a battle involving General Francis Marion, the Swamp Fox, during the Revolutionary War. It was burned during the Civil War and was never rebuilt.

I have wondered through the years about Biggin Church. Why was the church never rebuilt? What happened to the people who worshipped there? Why was this parish church allowed to die?

If the term *parish* isn't too strange a concept for us to deal with, I think it would be helpful to consider it as a concept that might help us come to grips with where we are in the American church today. As it relates to the church, a parish has two distinct but associated definitions. (1) A parish is a church district or territory. (2) A parish is the congregation or members of a church. As you can see, one definition is broad and denotes boundaries, and the other is more limited and connotes exclusivity. Both definitions are flawed from my perspective and factor into the decline and death of so many churches in America.

When churches operate from a boundaries mentality, they set up artificial parameters. This creates two fundamentally unbiblical realities: It puts limits on the church's mission, and it causes jealousy and conflict when other churches "trespass" on their territory. They become even more territorial and protective. Likewise, when churches operate from an exclusive mentality, they don't see beyond the walls of the church. It's all about what goes on inside the walls and those who "belong" there. Territory is not the issue. Arrogance is the issue.

The parish priest plays a role in this, of course. If he sees his parish in territorial terms, he exonerates himself from any responsibility or guilt about what happens beyond his district, real or imagined. In so doing, he excuses the church from any responsibility or guilt.

If he sees his parish in terms of members—those who belong—he becomes the consummate parish priest. He spends all his time and energy taking care of the sheep, his neatly packaged little flock of parishioners. He emphasizes to his people the importance of loving and serving one another. As long as he gives proper attention to his people, does not neglect the widows and the elderly, visits the sick, compassionately buries the dead, and joyfully baptizes the children, everyone's happy. As long as the people are happy, he feels satisfied and content with his work. He's done his job as a parish priest.

Yes, Baptists, Methodists, and Presbyterians—we are all parish priests one way or another, and our parishes are perishing!

In his eye-opening book, *The American Church in Crisis,* David T. Olson reports on an exhaustive study of the American church. He opens his book with these sobering words: "The American church is in crisis. At first glance this may not be apparent, but while many signs of its evident success and growth abound, in reality the American church is losing ground as the population continues to surge.... In reality the American church is not booming. It is in crisis. On any given Sunday, the vast majority of Americans are absent from church. Even more troublesome, as the American population continues to grow, the church falls further and further behind. If trends continue, by 2050 the percentage of Americans attending church will be half the 1990 figure" (David T. Olson, *The American Church in Crisis,* pp. 15,16).

Olson's book is the culmination of a twenty-year study called *The American Church Research Project,* which compiled some extensive data on the church in the United States from every state and every county in the nation. Attendance figures from over 200,000 Christian churches of all stripes were factored in. According to Olson, what comes out is not a pretty picture. It is a picture of a perishing world and a perishing parish.

In biblical parlance, the term *perish* is of profound significance as it relates to people. In some instances, it is used to describe physical death, as when the disciples were caught with Jesus in a furious storm and cried out to Jesus to rescue them, else they would "perish," or lose their lives. More significantly the word is used in reference to eternal death and the completion of spiritual destruction in contrast to eternal life. We are well familiar with Jesus' words to Nicodemus: "Whoever believes in him shall not *perish* but have eternal life." Jesus also gave this promise to believers: "My sheep listen to my voice; I know them, and they follow me. I give them eternal life, and they shall never *perish*; no one can snatch them out of my hand" (John 10:27–28).

The word also carries with it the meaning of being lost spiritually. Jesus prays in John 17 concerning the Twelve, "While I was with them, I protected them and kept them safe by the name you gave me. None has been *lost* except the one doomed to destruction so that the Scripture would be fulfilled."

The coming of Jesus was a rescue mission—a mission to rescue the perishing. That mission became the church's mission when it was launched in Jerusalem on the day of Pentecost and remains our mission until the Lord's return. Even in the first century, there were those who questioned why the Lord had not yet returned. Peter explains it like this: "The Lord is not slow in keeping his promise, as some understand slowness. He is patient with you, not wanting anyone to *perish*, but everyone to come to repentance" (2 Peter 3:9).

That is the heart of God and ought to be the heartbeat of the church. Our mission is to rescue the perishing of this world with the message of the cross, even though we know that there will be those who will not receive our message or us. "For the message of the cross is foolishness to those who are *perishing*, but to us who are being saved it is the power of God" (1 Cor. 1:18).

All great movements of God, spiritual awakenings, and periods of church renewal were accompanied by a vivid revelation of the perishing, a vision of the torment and pain of eternal death, and the anguish of an everlasting hell. This revelation always produced a passion in the church to be on mission with God to rescue the perishing from this destruction, because it gave new understanding to the unthinkable fate of those who are lost.

Church members checked their own spiritual pulses to see if they were alive or dead. Many discovered that they were still lost in their sins and were genuinely converted. Many turned their hearts toward their family members, neighbors, friends, and to foreign fields, because they were burdened to see everyone come to repentance and faith rather than go into eternity without Christ.

To a large degree, the American church has for decades ignored the biblical vision of hell in its preaching and teaching concerning the unfathomable horror that awaits the perishing. Ignoring the vision, we have lost that passion. Having lost the passion, our rescue mission is failing. And that's one major reason the church is failing.

What is happening in the American church is not dissimilar to what was happening in the church in England in the 1700s. It was a condition that disturbed an Anglican priest named John Wesley. Wesley was convinced the church was failing to call sinners to repentance and that it was ignoring the masses, which were perishing in their sins. Influenced greatly by his friend George Whitefield, Wesley was persuaded that the perishing could not be reached from the pulpit, so he took the message of the cross to the people. Many of these people were not the church kind, like the smudged-faced, dirty coal miners of his day, and others who were not normally welcomed in the parish churches.

While many people were brought to faith in these open-air meetings, Wesley had his critics in the church and endured intense opposition to his missional methods because, in part, he ignored parish boundaries. In response to this, Wesley wrote in his journal: "But, in the meantime, you think I ought to sit still; because otherwise I should invade another's office, if I interfered with other people's business and intermeddled with souls that did not belong to me. You accordingly ask, 'How is it that I assemble Christians who are none of my charge, to sing psalms, and pray, and hear the Scriptures expounded?' and I think it hard to justify doing this in other men's parishes, upon catholic principles?...

"I do not think it hard to do whatever I do. God in Scripture commands me, according to my power, to instruct the ignorant, reform the wicked, confirm the virtuous. Man forbids me to do this in another's parish; that is, in effect, to do it at all, seeing I have no parish of my own, nor probably ever shall. Whom then shall I hear, God or man? I look upon all the world as my parish; thus far I mean, that, in whatever part I am, I judge it meet, right, and my bounden duty to declare unto all that are willing to hear, the glad tidings of salvation."

Wesley, Whitefield, and others redefined the meaning of parish in their day, and it helped to usher in the First Great Awakening in America. Ignoring parish boundaries and church protocol, Whitefield, who had come to the colonies as an evangelist, led a spiritual movement characterized by the impassioned preaching of itinerate preachers who crisscrossed the colonial continent with the message of the cross. Lifeless and languishing churches of all denominations were enlivened, and large numbers of people were brought into the kingdom. Historians agree that the First Great Awakening not only gave shape to the American church, it also deeply affected American culture and society.

Could we not hope and pray for another awakening? Should we not come to a new understanding and redefinition of parish, ignoring as Wesley did, the entrenched parameters, prejudices, and protocol of our failing churches to reach the perishing?

That the American church is failing is undeniable. It is failing in more ways than one. It is failing to rescue the perishing in the world, especially right here in our own country and in our own communities. As Olson points out from the data, the gap between the surging population in our country and church attendance is ever widening. That means, of course, that more and more people in our country are without Christ and without hope in the world. They are perishing! That fact alone should break our hearts and burden our souls with an unprecedented missional motivation and passion.

However, there is another sense in which we must understand our perishing parish. Not only are people dying in their sins, but also churches are dying of their own maladies. Like old Biggin Church, they are left in ruins, no longer breathing or pulsing with life and vitality. The American Church Research Project discovered that in the decade of the 1990s, about 3200 churches ceased to function each year, amounting to approximately 32,000 churches over the decade—a staggering number. In addition, during the first decade of the new millennium, that number rose to about 3707 church closings a year.

Interestingly, Olson doesn't suggest we push the panic button over church closings, pointing out that though 32,000 closings during the 1990s seems like a pandemic running roughshod over our parishes, it actually represents only 1.1 percent per year of the total number of churches. As he explains, "One might expect that closures are quite common. Actually, they are not! Most churches are amazingly resilient. Very few older churches close over the course of a decade. Ask any denominational official who has encouraged a church to close, and you will hear a report of how feisty churches can be" (Olson, p. 119).

We applaud that spirit of survival. We commend stubbornness at death's door. However, it's one thing to be feisty, resilient, and resistant to death, but it's another thing altogether to be alive, healthy, growing, and effectively doing what New Testament churches are supposed to be doing—rescuing the perishing! There is a sense in which churches may not be at the point of death—that is, at the point of closure—but they are nonetheless perishing. They are perishing in the sense that they are in the process of dying. They are languishing, losing ground, losing members, and losing the vitality of being an influence in the community.

If it is true, as has been variously and widely reported, that somewhere around 85 to 90 percent of the churches in America are either in a prolonged state of stagnation or decline, the ramifications are enormous and more ominous than even church closures. As Olson suggests, this is a surprising conclusion drawn from the research. Church closures, while tragic and demoralizing, remain rather steady over time and do not figure in a significant way into the overall survival of the American church. The most crucial factor in the survival of the American church is the vitality of its existing churches and their ability to produce offspring.

Olson puts it to us like this: "For the church species to survive, three types of births are necessary. Is your church (or denomination) attracting and connecting with young adults and families so that there is a significant natural birthrate? Is your church (or denomination) seeing significant numbers of people become new followers of Jesus Christ? Is your church (or denomination) planting sizeable numbers of strong new churches?" (Olson, p. 124).

Here is where many of us who are pickled priests serving in our pickled parishes are struggling. In fact, if the reported data are anywhere near correct, then the vast majority of us are serving in parishes that are perishing. A few of us are probably gazing gloomily at the dark visage of death standing with its unholy hammer at the door of our church, ready to nail it shut forever.

The rest of us are wrestling with God about what we should do, how we should lead, and where we should go. We know our churches are perishing, even if death is not imminent. We know that we are seeing little in the way of new births. Our parishes are getting older, not just in years, but in the age of our parishioners. We have seen our younger families disappear over the last decade. We are seeing fewer and fewer in the way of new believers coming to faith in Christ. Attendance at best is holding steady, but is more than likely on the decline.

As pastors—the fruit of the boom—we are in a pickle. Everything we have understood about being a priest to God's people seems almost irrelevant anymore. Efforts to change the priorities, practices, policies, or protocol of our churches are met with stiff resistance from those who are "on our side," which inevitably produces in us a degree of resentment, frustration, and even anger. This, of course, only further hardens hearts and hastens the church's demise.

This is the problem, but there is a solution.

> "For the Lord watches over the way of the righteous,
> but the way of the wicked will perish."
>
> —PSALM 1:6

# CHAPTER TEN

# The Problem and the Solution

"In the year that King Uzziah died, I saw the
Lord seated on his throne, high and exalted."

—ISAIAH 6:1

The problem we face as pickled priests is that we are serving a pickled parish. Isaiah said it a different way, but the problem in his day was not unlike the problem of our day. He served in a day of cultural conflict, political corruption, and spiritual crisis. As a prophet of God, he was in personal crisis over the condition of his people. This personal spiritual crisis seems to have reached its zenith in the year that King Uzziah died, and Isaiah was given a life-altering vision of God, majestically and gloriously seated on his throne surrounded by heavenly beings declaring his holiness and ascribing him honor.

Isaiah was awestruck by the vision's reality. His heart and mind were overwhelmed with a sense of shame concerning his own guilt and the guilt of his people in the light of the holiness and majesty of God. In the sixth chapter, he records his desperate response. "'Woe to me!' I cried. 'I am ruined! For I am a man of unclean lips, and I live among a people of unclean lips, and my eyes have seen the King, the Lord Almighty.'"

The problem we have in many of our churches is that imperfect priests are trying to lead an imperfect people, and the parish is perishing. We are ruined! We've all become so saturated with the solution of vinegar, brine, and spices that we're pickled—preserved in the juices and spices of spiritual formation and culture. We don't do change, at least not well. What we do well is sit, soak, and sour. Our vision is blurred through the glass of our jar and the solution in which we live. So in a real sense, the problem is the "solution"! The problem is that we are all prisoners, trapped and in bondage to our own way of seeing, understanding, and living. I know I am, and I know that I serve a people just like me.

Now, there's a reason God gave Isaiah this special vision. This vision was to take away all the obstructions that existed in Isaiah's life that blurred his view of God so that he could see his own life as God saw him and his people. He became like Paul when the scales fell from his eyes. He had a new way of seeing things, and what he saw disgusted him. He saw himself as a man of unclean lips, living among a people of unclean lips. In other words, what they all said they believed was in stark contrast to what was in their hearts. They were pickled through and through, saturated in a solution of sin and tradition in the eyes of God. They couldn't see their own unrighteousness. So God gave Isaiah an unobstructed view of perfect holiness, and it rocked his world, propelling him to become the greatest of all the Old Testament prophets.

If the solution is the problem, then I would submit that the problem is the solution. In other words, Isaiah's personal spiritual crisis prepared him for the vision of God. Even in his sin and imperfection, he understood that there was a serious problem. "They honor me with their lips, but their hearts are far from me" (Isa. 29:13). And in the crucible of this personal and national crisis came a solution, the promise of renewal and restoration for his people.

The key to the solution is the vision. That is, the revelation of a current reality. For Isaiah, it was the motivation to meaningful action. "Here I am, send me." This revelation wasn't a vision of a fantasy, a fairytale future. It was a dramatic revelation of a sad state of affairs. It was also a revelation of some painful days ahead. It was a grim picture of judgment, destruction, and a perishing of the status quo.

> He said, "Go and tell this people: 'Be ever hearing, but never understanding; Be ever seeing, but never perceiving. Make the heart of this people calloused; make their ears dull and close their eyes. Otherwise they might see with their eyes,

hear with their ears, understand with their hearts, and turn and be healed.'" Then I said, "For how long, O Lord?" And he answered: "Until the cities lie ruined and without inhabitant, until the houses are left deserted and the fields ruined and ravaged, until the Lord has sent everyone far away and the land is utterly forsaken. And though a tenth remains in the land, it will again be laid waste. But as the terebinth and oak leave stumps when they are cut down, so the holy seed will be the stump in the land" (Isa. 6:9–13).

This is not a pretty picture for God's chosen people. What God has in store for them is some serious pruning. The Gardener is going to perform radical surgery. He's going to cut off branches that are nothing more than dead wood. It's going to be so drastic that nothing but a stump will be left. However, there is some good news in all this. God is not going to destroy the nation entirely. There will be a remnant, like the stump of an old oak tree, and new branches will grow from the old stump.

This was the promise of renewal and restoration for the chosen people. It was a promise that God made good on. But he threw something else in with this promise. It was an additional promise of a Savior who would rule over an everlasting kingdom of not just Jewish believers, but Gentile believers as well. The apostle Paul, the apostle to the Gentiles, explains God's eternal purposes in the judgment he brought upon the chosen people and the salvation he delivered to the Gentiles through Jesus. There's an important message here for the church today.

Again I ask: Did they stumble so as to fall beyond recovery? Not at all! Rather, because of their transgression, salvation has come to the Gentiles to make Israel envious. But if their transgression means riches for the world, and their loss means riches for the Gentiles, how much greater riches will their fullness bring.

I am talking to you Gentiles. Inasmuch as I am the apostle to the Gentiles, I make much of my ministry in the hope that I may somehow arouse my own people to envy and save some of them. For if their rejection is the reconciliation of the world, what will their acceptance be but life from the dead? If the part of the dough offered as firstfruits is holy, then the whole batch is holy; if the root is holy, so are the branches.

If some of the branches have been broken off, and you, though a wild olive shoot, have been grafted in among the others and now share in the nourishing sap from the olive root, do not boast over those branches. If you do, consider this: You do not support the root, but the root supports you. You will say then, 'Branches were broken off so that I could be grafted in.' Granted. But they were broken off because of unbelief, and you stand by faith. Do not be arrogant, but be afraid. For if God did not spare the natural branches, he will not spare you either (Rom. 11:11–21).

This is a sobering truth for the American church today because there is a lot of arrogance in the church. Paul confronts our arrogance with the truth that if God did not hesitate to cut off the branches of the natural olive tree, that is the Jews, he will certainly not hesitate to cut off the branches of the wild olive tree (Gentile believers), which have been grafted into the living stump.

It seems to me that we are living in a time of judgment on the wild olive tree in America, and God has begun cutting off the dead wood. There is a painful period ahead for the church, as the lifeless branches of the wild olive are removed to give way to the new growth that is already emerging. It is not within our power, nor is it our responsibility to engineer these changes. Jesus said, "I will build my church." It is our responsibility to be vessels of God's Spirit and servants ready to do his bidding. When God asks, "Who will go for us? Who will be my servants?" those who answer like Isaiah—"Here I am. Send me!"—he will send.

God doesn't need us to preserve the church in its present state. God doesn't need us to defend the church. Our inclination as pickled priests is to do the same thing the priests did with Jesus and his revelation—fight it. The Father is always working to transform his people, pruning the dead and giving opportunity for new life to appear. The fact is, God doesn't need us at all, but he will use those who are willing to partner with him in the work of the coming kingdom.

I look at First Baptist, and I wonder what's ahead for her. For twenty years I've confidently, maybe arrogantly, counted on hard work, ingenious programs, and attempts at becoming "contemporary" to usher in that growth and excitement I've longed for and prayed for as pastor. Promises of remarkable population growth, the addition of important industrial investments, and an anticipated business boom in our area have not quite materialized. In our planning, we put a great deal of emphasis on what we believed was a sure thing. We were going to see a period of unprecedented growth. We were going to finally leave the plateau we'd been sitting on for so long. We have been largely disappointed and some are disillusioned. It just hasn't happened.

In the remaining years I have left to serve this church, I now see my role in a much different light. I now see my role as one of preparing our people for an immense transformation. I view it as my responsibility to prepare the church for some painful but necessary changes and to help them see how God is working in the midst of these changes over which we have no control, to restore and renew his people.

I am beginning to grasp what Reggie McNeil is saying in his book, *The Present Future,* when he talks about the difference between planning and preparing. He writes, "The difference between planning and preparedness is more than semantics in the biblical teaching. God does the planning; we do the preparing. It is God who declares: 'I know the plans I have for you,' he says in Jeremiah 29:11. He does not say, 'I am waiting on you to develop plans I can bless.' I am not against planning. I am just suggesting that there is a dimension beyond planning that is critical for us to understand. We can settle for our imaginations, our plans, and our dreams. In fact, I think the North American church has done just that. We have the best churches people can plan and build. But we are desperate for God to show up and do something that only he can get credit for. God wants us to pray and to prepare for his intervention. God knows, we need it" (Reggie McNeil, *The Present Future,* p. 95).

I am one of many pastors across America in similar situations. We serve in churches we have planned and built. They are good churches, but little that is supernatural is taking place. We can take credit for that. Many of us are confused and discouraged. I understand. Many of us are weary and worn. I understand. We have given our best effort with little to show for it. I understand. We find ourselves in the midst of a crisis, and we don't know what to do next.

Perhaps we should consider that we're right where God wants us. Maybe we should regard this crisis as a unique opportunity. The problem might just be the solution. In the crisis, God gives us a revelation. It's a revelation of purging and pruning that leads to restoration and renewal, and we are in the very strategic position of leading our churches to embrace this vision and prepare them for what's ahead.

Unless God gives us a John-like revelation and allows us to see what will soon take place, we don't really know what's ahead in clear, specific terms. I have no clue what First Baptist will look like in 2020 (an ironic number as it relates to vision), but I can help prepare First Baptist for what the Lord, the Head of the body, will do to make his bride "holy, cleansing her by the washing with water through the word, and to present her to himself as a radiant church, without stain or wrinkle or any other blemish, but holy and blameless" (Eph. 5:26–27).

Look, fellow priests. The Lord is on his throne in all his glory. Listen, my fellow pastors. The Lord is asking, "Who will go for us?" Do you see that we are pickled priests living in the midst of a pickled people? How will we respond? What is our answer? Let us answer with a collective cry, "Here we are. Send us! Send us with the message you have given us. Send us anew with the message to our perishing parish. Send us with the message of Jesus, the root of Jesse. Send us with the message of the cross, even though we know it is "foolishness to those who are perishing, but to those of us who are being saved it is the power of God" (1 Cor. 1:18).

How we go about preparing our parishes for what's ahead begins with how we prepare ourselves. We must rediscover ourselves. We are so programmed, pickled in the solution of our church culture, that we're struggling mightily with our own identity and calling in Christ. I believe we have to do four things: (1) We must reexamine our call. (2) We must reawaken our passion. (3) We must recast our vision. (4) We must redefine our parish.

## Reexamining Our Call

More than once I've volunteered for something and found myself in the middle of a mess, wondering silently, "What am I doing here, and why did I ever say yes to this?" It happens in ministry too.

It's a healthy, helpful exercise from time to time to revisit our calling. I've done that through the years. Most of the time it's just a fond remembrance. However, there have been a few times when doubt or discouragement forced me to retreat to that very real call of God to reaffirm that his hand was upon me and that his call was still in affect.

Reexamining our call is a little different, I think. It assumes that our call is certain and not in question. Instead, it gets at the core question: "What exactly has God called me to do?" Some might say, "He called me to preach the Word!" Others might say, "He called me to pastor a church." There might be a few who would respond, "He called me to win souls for Jesus." I wouldn't argue with any of those responses, but it seems to me that those responses might be a bit narrow in scope and shallow in understanding.

I just took a moment to gaze at some now-fading certificates, both encased in black frames, hanging prominently but mostly ignored, on my study wall. I wonder, "When was the last time I took a look at those things?" It's been a while.

I took them down and laid them on my desk. I studied them carefully. I read the words, "Certificate of License. This is to certify that Harold N. West, Jr., who has given evidence that God has called him into The Gospel Ministry, was licensed to preach the Gospel as he may have opportunity, and to exercise his gifts in the work of ministry."

Then I read the other, which says, "Certificate of Ordination. We the undersigned, hereby certify that upon the recommendation and request of the First Baptist Church at Moncks Corner, South Carolina, which had full and sufficient opportunity for judging his gifts, and after satisfactory examination by us in regard to his Christian experience, call to the ministry, and views of Bible doctrine, Harold N. West, Jr. was solemnly and publicly set apart and ordained to the work of the Gospel Ministry."

I had always understood "the Gospel Ministry" in terms of the traditional role of pastor, which included preaching, teaching, and pastoral ministry to a certain flock, providing comfort, counseling, and care to those who might call me to serve them as their pastor. Unfortunately, many of us in "the Gospel Ministry" today see our calling in terms of *church work,* which is not wrong. It's just inadequate, and it's no wonder we feel so ill-equipped at this point in our ministry when so much has changed since we accepted the call with genuine humility and enormous desire to serve the Lord.

For most of us, the problem is not our call, but our incomplete understanding of the call. At its core, the call to the gospel ministry is a call to complete surrender and service to the Lord Jesus Christ. When we said yes to God, we were saying yes to anything the Lord commands us to do and agreeing go anywhere the Lord directs us to go. We accepted the responsibility of becoming a fellow-laborer with him in world redemption.

We've run into the present crisis because, while God is marching through time ushering in his kingdom, we're still stuck in the model and motif of ministry that was more suited to a past era, and is inadequate for the present.

Reggie McNeil addresses this issue and offers the challenge to a new kind of leadership. "A new breed of church leader has been emerging that will meet the leadership challenges of what it will take for the church to become more missionally effective. In the last decades of the twentieth century, a new leadership genus began appearing on the North American scene. The leadership type is what I and others have dubbed 'Apostolic leadership.' This connotation seems appropriate primarily because the challenges to church leaders in the emerging twenty-first century parallel those that faced leaders in the first Christian century (commonly called the apostolic era). These include religious pluralism, globalism, and the collapse of institutional religion, accompanied by an increased interest in personal spiritual development. The focus of apostolic leadership is not on office or gifts (these are how people in the church culture deal with the term *apostle*), but on the content of leadership that responds to the new spiritual landscape by shaping a church movement that more resembles the world of Acts than America in the last half of the twentieth century" (Reggie McNeil, *The Present Future*, p. 125–126).

Many of us have bemoaned the fact that our church members are resistant to change, but the more important issue here is our own reluctance to change, pickled as we are in the solution of the church culture of our recent past. In reevaluating our call, we must ask ourselves when we stopped keeping in step with the Spirit of God and why we are so slow to obey and serve the Master where he is working. Are we now ready to just coast along to the end of our careers, content to maintain our anemic programs for our dwindling flock with the idea of letting somebody else deal with the perishing parish? Or are we so discontented with the current state of affairs that we are more than ready and willing to embrace this challenge with a fresh infusion of passion to both follow the Lord and lead our people to be on a mission with God? That is a matter of calling, and calling is a matter of obedience and surrender.

## Reawakening Our Passion

A passionless, pickled priest cannot awaken the passionless, pickled parish. It just won't happen. But think about how, in one way or another, you have pleaded with your people to be a people of passion and have prayed to the Almighty to awaken your people. Could it be that both the people and the Almighty find your pleas and your prayers hollow because both know that you lost your passion a long time ago, and you are the last to realize it?

What happens to us is somewhat like what happened to my brother John—my long-time hunting partner—and me this past duck hunting season. We arrived at the hunting cabin before sunrise one December morning with our boat in tow. We stepped into the cabin to speak to our friends, exchanged a cold morning's warm greetings, and then headed back out to the truck. It was then that I decided to do something I thought was rather clever at the time, but turned out to be quite dumb. Beneath the glow of the outdoor cabin light, I easily untied the bowline that fastened the boat to the trailer, thinking that this maneuver would expedite our launch at the landing. It was always a chore to untie that line in the dark with cold hands.

I slowly drove down the causeway that separated two large rice fields, vestiges from a long-ago Southern culture, which now served the sports of fishing and hunting. Reaching the edge of the Cooper River, I turned along the river bank on a tree-lined road toward another causeway from which we would launch our little duck boat. Daylight was nearing, and I hurriedly got out of the truck only to face a shocking reality. "John!" I shouted. "The boat's gone!"

We retreated hastily back down the riverbank looking intently for our lost cargo. Soon we noticed the headlights of a line of trucks stopped on the main causeway. I knew we were in for an embarrassing encounter with some fellow hunters. A few moments later, we saw it. The boat rested harmlessly in the middle of the road. Standing by was one of our oldest friends, a retired dentist, who was relishing this moment like a mouth full of cavities. "Have you lost something?" he asked with both noticeable sarcasm and glee.

I wonder if somewhere in the course of our ministry, in our haste to expedite the Lord's work or to make it easy, we have outsmarted ourselves and lost a necessary spiritual commodity—passion. And I wonder if there are those behind us whose paths are blocked and they're waiting on us to make this self-discovery. I wonder if they are relishing an opportunity to ask us the question: "Have you lost something?"

About a year ago, I told two trusted confidants of mine that I still had fire in my bones. Looking back, I wonder if was just my arthritis flaring up again. Reawakening personal spiritual passion means being renewed in one's own relationship with Jesus. You and Jesus are tight, I'm sure. You've been walking with him for years. And yet, if you were honest, you might have to admit that the relationship is missing something. It's missing passion. In the daily grind and weekly whirlwind, you lost it. It happens in the strongest relationships. You don't intend for it to happen. It just happens. It happens in all of our closest relationships.

In this critical time in your ministry and in the life of the church, nothing is more important than reawakening your passion for Jesus. With that in mind, I suggest to you what a good friend of mine suggested to me: Take some time away from the monotony of ministry and get alone with God. Concentrate on your own personal relationship with him. He understands.

Let's think for a moment about Simon Peter. If any disciple was a likely candidate for burnout and lost passion, it would be Peter. He was a high-octane kind of guy, hard driving and task oriented. He was a real go-getter, as we say. Remember, at the transfiguration it was Peter who offered to build three shelters for Jesus, Moses, and Elijah. He was a fisherman, not a shepherd. He was more occupational than relational. He took failure very hard.

When Peter bailed out on Jesus during the crisis of the cross, he suffered from guilt and shame. He struggled with a deep sense of inadequacy. Alone with Jesus during one of those short post-resurrection appearances of Jesus, he was given an opportunity to renew his relationship with the Lord in the afterglow of the resurrection. Jesus took him aside for a heart-to-heart conversation and asked him a very direct question: "Do you love me?" In fact, as you know, he asked Peter the question three times, each time penetrating a little deeper into the core of his being, piercing beneath the pain and shame of his sense of failure. I don't think Jesus was after the answer to that question for himself, but for Peter. I think Jesus was taking Peter to a place of self-discovery and revelation. I think Jesus was teaching Peter that relationship is more important that success or failure.

When Jesus had succeeded in taking Peter to that inner place where passion is pure, the message became clear. "Feed my sheep." Later, with the Holy Spirit's empowerment on the day of Pentecost, Peter became a man possessed—a man possessed with both power and passion.

You may think it counterintuitive to take some time away from your duties while so many responsibilities await you and demand your attention. You may be convinced that you cannot afford the luxury of such a personal retreat. You might even feel guilty just considering such a thing. But consider this: can you afford not to? Do you want to continue to struggle as Peter must have struggled with his failure and inadequacies?

I would urge you to take some time to renew your relationship with Jesus. It's the only way to reawaken your spiritual passion. At a minimum, take a week away from the church. If at all possible, take two. Better yet, if you have some tenure to justify it, take a sabbatical leave of one to three months. Whatever amount of time you can carve out for this one-on-one with Jesus, take it and use it. There is something powerful about getting alone with the resurrected Lord.

Stop feeling guilty about this. It's not about what you deserve or don't deserve. This is not a vacation or a reward for service. This is about reawakening your passion so that you can serve the Lord with resurrection power again. This is not a time to write sermons, plan your calendar, or map out some strategy. This is a time of intense soul-searching and self-examination. "Have I lost my passion? Where did I lose it? Why have I lost it? Do I love Jesus? Do I *really* love Jesus?" This is a time of prayer, meditation, confession, and introspection. This is a time to listen to the voice of Jesus, allowing him to take you on a journey to the center of your soul.

In this process of self-discovery, the Lord may well reveal to you some sin or sins that have long been hidden or forgotten that may be hindrances to your ministry or, more importantly, barriers in your relationship with Jesus. Confess them and repent immediately. Like David, pray, "Restore to me the joy of your salvation" (Ps. 51:12). That joy is passion. You might discover a pattern of thinking and a way of seeing things that is not the mind of Christ. Pray with David, "Search me, O God, and know my heart; test me and know my anxious thoughts. See if there is any offensive way in me, and lead me in the way that is everlasting" (Ps. 139:23–24).

We've all prayed that prayer many times, but have we ever spent time letting God deal with us on what that prayer is really saying? You might discover that you have become a slave to ministry rather than a prisoner of the Lord Jesus Christ. There's an important difference. Self-discovery can set you free. You might be living under a dark cloud of discouragement or even a long shadow of disillusionment. Time spent in the Light will expose everything that is hanging over your head or blocking the sunlight of his love for you. In the light of his infinite love, you will be renewed in your passion for him. It is then that you will understand the words, "Feed my sheep."

## Recasting the Vision

We value the prophet who tells it like it is, and we strive to be that preacher who proclaims the Word with uncompromising boldness, don't we? We love it when someone commends our preaching with something like, "That's what I like to hear, Preacher. Tell it like it is!"

Let's be real. Do we really tell it like is? We have more sermon material than we know what to do with. The current culture and the blatant sins of society provide ample fodder for our Sunday rants—godless humanism, greedy materialism, media filth, eroding values, and runaway immorality. The enemy has made himself an easy target. How clever he is! The more he diverts our attention, and the more we attack the symptoms of our sick society, the less we address the maladies of the body of Christ.

Feeding the sheep isn't feeding them the poison pill of disdain for our perishing world—the same world that Jesus came and died to redeem. That is not to say that we shouldn't tell it like it is regarding the ungodliness of our society and that which calls for the judgment of God. But it *is* to say that the message of divine wrath against a godless world alone is not the whole truth and does not feed the sheep.

We delude ourselves and our sheep with the mindset that while the rest of the world is going to hell, we're doing just fine. We deceive ourselves and our people by continuing to cast a vision of a bright and glorious day to come, oblivious to the real truth that is staring us in the face. We look in the wrong direction when we try to peer into the future and pretend to pierce the veil that separates today from tomorrow. It's a form of arrogance. Proverbs 27:1 cautions, "Do not boast about tomorrow, for you do not know what a day may bring forth."

What we can do, and what we must do, is to look up and squint in awe at the glory and majesty of the Most High God and look into his eyes at the reflection of what we really are. What we see is the revelation, the heavenly vision, of an American church that is arrogant, self-righteous, self-sufficient, boastful, human-driven, and materialistically empowered. We will see a reflection of our own culture similar to Paul's description in 2 Timothy 3:1–5.

> But mark this: There will be terrible times in the last days. People will be lovers of themselves, lovers of money, boastful, proud, abusive, disobedient to their parents, ungrateful, unholy, without love, unforgiving, slanderous, without self-control, brutal, not lovers of the good, treacherous, rash, conceited, lovers of pleasure rather than lovers of God—having a form of godliness but denying its power. Have nothing to do with them.

The cultural Christianity of our day will never substantially change society. There is no salt in it. It produces very little light. For all its bluster, it continues to embrace the very culture it decries. To tell it like it is, is to tell it like the true prophets of the Scripture, whose primary message was to God's own people, calling them to account. It was the cold, hard truth.

To reclaim our redemptive role in the world, we must recast a vision of the present reality, preparing God's people for the pruning that has already begun, holding out the promise of renewal and restoration that is the heart of our holy God and our righteous Savior. I began to understand this about a year ago. I don't know how it will turn out, but I began to prepare our staff, deacons, and other leaders with the vision of the present reality about nine months ago.

I am carefully, methodically recasting this vision to the church. I am praying that together we will grasp the glory of what we see in the majesty and holiness of God, that we will courageously and humbly peer into the eyes of God and see what he sees. I am praying that we will rightly perceive the depth and breadth of the present crisis, and that in self-surrender and repentance the Spirit of God will move us to answer the high calling of God in Christ Jesus. The problem is the solution.

## Redefining Our Parish

Historically, the church has been at its best when times were at their worst. When the culture has been a crucible of suffering for believers, when persecution has put the faithful to the test or the sword has put them to death, when the church itself has been disciplined by the righteous rod of God, the true church emerges with purity, power, and beauty. Furthermore, God's eternal purposes in the redeemed are manifest in the expansion and growth of the church and the transformation of lives, villages, cities, and societies. The history of the Christian movement provides ample evidence of this phenomenon.

We see it in the first church, the church in Jerusalem. On the day of Pentecost, the transformation began. It began with the remarkable transformation of the believers gathered in the upper room. From there it spreads in unprecedented power to the city, with the conversion of three thousand souls. Some who were converted that day were Jewish pilgrims from faraway places who had come to Jerusalem for the festivities, not coincidentally. Almost certainly, the gospel began to spread across that part of the ancient world through the witness of these new believers.

As the days unfolded, the apostles displayed the power of God in their lives and words, and the church grew by the thousands. This didn't happen quietly. What happened was what the Jewish leaders had feared would happen; but they had no way of knowing just how powerful this movement would become, and the church came under attack. You know the story well. After the death of Stephen, the Scripture says, "On that day a great persecution broke out against the church at Jerusalem, and all except the apostles were scattered throughout Judea and Samaria" (Acts 8:1).

Luke tells us later that they went further than that. "Now those who had been scattered by the persecution in connection with Stephen traveled as far as Phoenicia, Cyprus, and Antioch, telling the message only to the Jews. Some of them, however, men from Cyprus and Cyrene, went to Antioch and began to speak to Greeks also, telling them the good news about the Lord Jesus. The Lord's hand was with them, and a great number of people believed and turned to the Lord" (Acts 11:19–21).

The Lord used this time of great persecution in Jerusalem to expand his work beyond the geographical parameters of Jerusalem and beyond the human parameters of race, ethnicity, and social status. He didn't waste any time in demonstrating his intent in the Great Commission. He was quick to reassert that the world was his parish.

The Jerusalem church, the world's first mega church, had it going. The Spirit was working mightily through the believers, and the city was being transformed in miraculous ways. Nevertheless, they did not possess a worldwide vision for the gospel. It took a special meeting with Paul and Barnabas to convince them that the Lord was really moving in the hearts and lives of the Gentiles in other places, like Antioch and beyond.

The danger for the Jerusalem church was in having a very narrow understanding and perception of their parish. That is one reason God gave Peter that vision in Acts 10 that led to his encounter with Cornelius, where, as he was speaking, "the Holy Spirit came on all who heard the message." The Scripture says that the Jewish believers who had accompanied Peter to Cornelius' house "were astonished that the gift of the Holy Spirit had been poured out even on the Gentiles" (Acts 10:45).

I think the danger for us is similar. The danger for us as parish priests is to have a very narrow understanding and perception of our parish. We tend to think of our parish as those who belong to our church, and we spend our time and energy ministering to them. We become very inwardly focused in a way that diminishes our evangelistic opportunities and our missional mandate.

We must redefine our parish in more missional terms. Our parish is more than those who belong to us. In sending his Son, the Father defined our parish. "For God so loved the world that he gave his one and only Son, that whoever believes in him shall not perish but have eternal life" (John 3:16). Our parish is defined by the life, death, and resurrection of Jesus. "All this is from God, who reconciled us to himself through Christ and gave us the ministry of reconciliation: that God was reconciling the world to himself in Christ, not counting men's sins against them. And he has committed to us the message of reconciliation" (2 Cor. 5:18–19).

As pastors of churches that have, over years or even decades, become inwardly focused, it is imperative that we redefine our parish to include the perishing. Otherwise, we perish ourselves. Today, more and more pastors are leading their churches to become what is being called "missional" churches. These are churches that have redefined their parish. They are engaging the culture, connecting with their community, and leading their members to become missionaries according to the Acts 1:8 model and the Great Commission mandate. And these are the churches that are going to be a prominent part of the movement of God in the twenty-first century.

While new churches, which are not so encumbered with history and tradition, are in a better position to be missional from the start, we can't rely on new churches alone to get the job done. Starting new churches is an imperative. But it is equally imperative for older churches to make that very difficult transition from being a parish church, which is itself perishing, to being a church which communicates and connects with a perishing world. As pastors, we play a crucial role in redefining our parish in these days of crisis. This responsibility is critical to both a perishing parish and a perishing world. The problem is the solution.

Now comes the hard part. Rediscovering your identity and your calling in Christ may be a challenge, but that's the easy part compared to addressing the greater challenge of preparing your church to extract and transfer itself from the church-culture solution into a missional modality.

All churches are not created equal. Each is unique and presents its own peculiar set of conditions. Some churches are more entrenched than others. Some are rigidly structured and governed by a long-standing, written constitution and by-laws and other policy and procedures that make substantial changes hard to initiate and navigate. There are so many steps in the process that, at any point, an initiative of substance might get bogged down in a committee or board. You might begin the process with great enthusiasm and support, but after months of meetings and long discussions that lead to nowhere, momentum is lost and, many times, the opportunity as well.

In some churches, the power structure is in the hands of a few—a board, committee, deacons, elders, officers, certain families, or certain individuals of intrinsic influence. Typically, these are people who are by nature resistant to change and champions of the status quo. They hold the "keys to the kingdom" and decide what to hold on to and what to let go of, including the pastor. It takes a great deal of wisdom, skill, courage, and patience to effect change under those circumstances.

Some churches are so pickled you couldn't squeeze the vinegar out of them with a steamroller. They are so anchored in the past, they don't even know that the tide has gone out. With the waters of the twentieth-century church culture receding, they are sitting high and dry, still rowing frantically, but futilely going nowhere.

Moving churches such as these will require supernatural intervention. If you are the pastor of one of these churches, there is good news and bad news. The bad news is that it is impossible for you to succeed in facilitating any substantial change. The good news in those situations is that you can realize your total dependence on God. You can abandon any confidence in your own ability and know-how and believe with all your heart that with God nothing is impossible.

On the other hand, there are some churches that are more ready and willing to listen to and follow godly leadership. But whether you lead a church entrenched in the past or one that is ready to move forward, you must lead them with passion and vision. You cannot do it alone, nor should you. The whole point of your calling as a priest/prophet is to lead people in becoming partners with God and with you in the gospel ministry.

To accomplish this requires some creativity on our part. Here's where we must tap into God's holy imagination and divine creativity. We should set three primary goals: (1) Create a partnership with our people in the gospel ministry. (2) Cultivate a passion in our people for the perishing. (3) Construct a pathway for our people to become missionaries.

## Creating a Partnership with Our People

I love what Paul says in his letter to the believers in Philippi. More than any other letter Paul wrote to the churches, the letter to the Philippians reveals the softer side of the apostle Paul. He has great affection for this early church that was born out of a prayer meeting and an earthquake during his second missionary journey. He has great admiration and respect for them because, even in their hardship and poverty, they gave money to his missionary enterprise. They were *missional* is the purest sense of this now-popular catchword. From a Roman jail, Paul writes:

> I thank my God every time I remember you. In all my prayers for all of you, I always pray with joy because of your partnership in the gospel from the first day until now, being confident of this, that he who began a good work in you will carry it on to completion until the day of Christ Jesus. It is right for me to feel this way about all of you, since I have you in my heart; for whether I am in chains or defending and confirming the gospel, all of you share in God's grace with me. God can testify how I long for all of you with the affection of Christ Jesus (Phil. 1:3–8).

Certainly, Paul loved all the churches, but he loved these people with all the affection of Christ. And we must, in the same way, love the people we serve and lead as well. But in serving them and leading them, we must form not only a bond of love but also a bond of partnership, a partnership in the gospel. Our ministry is hollow and ineffectual without that strong partnership between us. It is arrogant and foolish to think that we can move our churches toward restoration and renewal without forging a true partnership in the gospel ministry.

You should start small and work outward. Identify the small group of influencers in the body. Engage them in an honest dialogue, and begin to reveal your vision and passion. Give them your frank assessment of the church based on the Scripture and the current facts. Tell them what's at stake for the church and for your perishing parish. Avoid coming across as a panicky pastor, but let them feel your passion. Let them process, ask questions, and "play the devil's advocate." Listen to their questions, and receive and value their input and perspective. At this point, your goal is not to solve all the problems, but to form an alliance of leaders and a bond of partnership.

Patiently pray with and stay with these leaders, until you believe there is a significant meeting of the minds and joining of hearts—a unity of the

Spirit in the bond of peace. Then begin to broaden the circle, bringing others into a wider discussion. Finally, after serious prayer and preparation on your part, do some of your best, Spirit-filled teaching and preaching, challenging your whole church to partner together in the gospel ministry with a unity of purpose.

## Cultivating a Passion in Your People

True spiritual passion is born of revelation. It's not a passing emotion. You don't get over it. It burns in your soul and moves you with energy and zeal no matter what the cost, without regard to reward or acclaim.

Paul's passion came from the revelation of that heavenly vision that first blinded his eyes and pierced his heart. The zeal he ignorantly possessed for the Law was transformed into a passion that possessed him for the gospel. In 1 Corinthians, he was defending his rights as an apostle to receive monetary support from the churches. But he says this: "But I have not used any of these rights. And I am not writing this in the hope that you will do such things for me. I would rather die than have anyone deprive me of this boast. Yet when I preach the gospel, I cannot boast, for I am compelled to preach. Woe to me if I do not preach the gospel!" (1 Cor. 9:15–16).

Jeremiah was "burdened" with God's call and revelation. It was a burden that he found overwhelming. In Jeremiah 20, he pours out his complaint to the Lord. He must have been at a point of total despair, because he accuses the Lord of bullying him into service. He resents being ridiculed and threatened. But then he says, "But if I say, 'I will not mention him or speak anymore in his name,' his word (his revelation) is in my heart like a fire, a fire shut up in my bones. I am weary of holding it in; indeed, I cannot" (Jer. 20:9). Jeremiah had a passion for the Word of the Lord even if it was a reluctant passion. That fire in his bones came through revelation.

Speaking of bones, God gave Ezekiel a vision of a valley of dry bones in Ezekiel 37:

He asked me, "Son of man, can these bones live?"

I said, "O Sovereign Lord, you alone know."

Then he said to me, "Prophesy to these dry bones and say to them, 'Dry bones, hear the word of the Lord! This is what the Sovereign Lord says to these bones: I will make breath enter you, and you will come to life. I will attach tendons to you and make flesh come upon you and cover you with skin; I will put breath in you, and you will come to life. Then you will know that I am the Lord.'"

So I prophesied as I was commanded. And as I was prophesying, there was a noise, a rattling sound, and the bones came together, bone to bone. I looked, and tendons and flesh appeared on them, but there was no breath in them.

Then he said to me, "Prophesy to the breath; prophesy, son of man, and say to it, 'This is what the Sovereign Lord says: "Come from the four winds, O breath, and breath into these slain, that they may live."'" So I prophesied as he commanded me, and breath entered them; they came to life and stood on their feet—a vast army.

Then he said to me: "Son of man, these bones are the whole house of Israel. They say, 'Our bones are dried up and our hope is gone; we are cut off'" (Ezek. 37:3–11).

What a picture of the power of the Sovereign Lord this is! It is a picture of a promise to bring new life to the spiritually dead—life that only God himself can give. Could this vision of the valley of dry bones not also be a picture of many of our churches today? It's a picture of lifelessness, but it's also a revelation of hope and renewal. The Lord tells Ezekiel to tell the people: "I will put my Spirit in you and you will live" (Ezek. 37:14). Just when many are ready to bury the bones of the church, we as pastors need to passionately proclaim, "Not so fast! Cancel the funeral procession. These bones can live!"

Ezekiel describes these resurrected bones as a vast army. I believe this is exactly what the Lord is doing in the current American church. The Gardener is cutting off the dead branches, pruning the church, and transforming the body of Christ. He's going to renew the church with resurrection power, filling it with new life and new passion, creating a vast army for the kingdom.

No one is going to compare us with Paul, Jeremiah, Ezekiel, or any of the great prophets and apostles of Scripture. Nonetheless, if our passion is awakened and that fire is rekindled in our bones, there is a much better chance for that passion to be reborn in our people.

It has been said that enthusiasm is contagious. There's some truth to that statement. Human emotions are easily manipulated. All you have to do is analyze the sports world, where enthusiasm can reach a feverish level; or examine the political process where certain candidates can quickly amass a large, boisterous following. But understand this: enthusiasm and passion are not the same. True spiritual passion is not contagious. Passion is not something you can catch by exposure. Enthusiasm is viral; it's a twenty-four- or forty-eight-hour bug. Passion is born of the Spirit. It is the seed of the new birth and renewal that bears the fruit of the Holy Spirit's fire—fire in the bones that cannot be mistaken for an arthritis flare-up.

How then does a spiritual leader cultivate passion in his people if he cannot infect them with his own passion? Again, passion comes from revelation, so that a spiritual leader must communicate a vision that will stir passion in the hearts of the people. That vision, as we have said, is one of both current crisis and future promise. The false, empty vision of a bright and beautiful future may create enthusiasm, but it will quickly fade into a lukewarm malaise, while the current crisis is unacknowledged and ignored. Truth is liberating, on the other hand, and stirs the heart to repentance and obedience to the Lord who freely pardons and fills with passion.

This passion, when it is full-blown, is directed in three continuous and connected directions. It is a passion characterized by a holistic love for God. It continues in the power of godly love toward the body of Christ, the church. At its fullest expression, this passion is directed toward the perishing. Said another way, this three-directional passion expresses itself in authentic worship, self-sacrificial ministry and fellowship, and Spirit-empowered evangelism and missions.

This may sound purpose-driven, but it is not driven by purpose. It is a way of life that is passion-driven. It is purpose driven by passion. It is the difference between enthusiasm and passion. But ultimately, if passion doesn't create a missional mindset in your people, it falls short of its purpose as God intended it.

## Constructing a Pathway for Our People

It has been famously said that Charleston, South Carolina, is located where the Ashley and Cooper Rivers meet to form the Atlantic Ocean. As a life-long low-country resident, I would have to admit that this is a bit of an exaggeration. Charleston is also famously nicknamed "the Holy City" because its skyline is prominently painted with the spires of its historic downtown churches. This too is more than a little hyperbolic.

Along with the beautiful steeples of Charleston, there is a recent addition to the skyline that has added to the charm and beauty of this unique port city—the twin cabled towers of the new Copper River Bridge, officially known as the Arthur Ravenel Jr. Bridge, which was opened to traffic in July 2005 with great fanfare and celebration. This fabulous bridge consists of eight twelve-foot lanes, four in each direction, connecting Mt. Pleasant to Charleston along Highway 17, a major highway of the southeastern coast.

Because of the large population growth of the Charleston/Mt. Pleasant areas, the expanding port demands on the infrastructure, and the burgeoning tourism traffic, a new bridge was desperately needed. There were already two older bridges connecting Charleston and Mt. Pleasant, but these bridges were both old and insufficient to meet traffic demands and public safety. The oldest bridge, the Grace Memorial Bridge, was built in 1929 and was a real safety concern.

It was amazing to watch as the new bridge took shape during its four-year construction span. All of us in the low country watched as the new bridge rose above and around the old bridges. It was also amazing to observe the old bridges being meticulously deconstructed after the new bridge was completed.

As pastors and church leaders, we live in a time of outdated and insufficient pathways that will take us over the great divide that exists between the church and the perishing world. The gap seems to be widening in America where the population is expanding at a faster rate than the church is making new disciples. We have to come to grips with the fact that the old bridges are outdated and insufficient. We desperately need to construct new bridges and new pathways to connect us to our perishing parish.

While an awakened church with renewed passion will give us the zeal we need to reach out to the perishing, it is imperative that we as pastors and church leaders provide these new bridges, new avenues, and new opportunities by which we can lead our people to connect with our mission field.

The thing about a bridge is that it opens up a two-way opportunity, but in the past, the church saw the old bridges as a one-way deal. We saw these old bridges as a way the perishing could connect with the church. We built our bridges and our buildings and our programs with the mindset that the perishing would come to us; and to a degree, it worked. But it's not working today, and it isn't the New Testament church at its best. The New Testament church at its best is a church on mission, a church that has been sent and goes to the perishing world. We must build new bridges that we see as our pathways to the community and to the world.

One of the great problems we are dealing with is that we in the church have become so out-of-touch with the community in which we exist. We have become strangers in our own hometown. We don't know our neighbors. We are oblivious to the pockets of people who are perishing in both poverty and prosperity. We are practically isolated from the people to whom we have been sent. As strange as it may sound, we are compelled to rediscover our own parish.

This is, in part, the message of the excellent book by Ed Stetzer and David Putman. In *Breaking the Missional Code,* these authors make a compelling case for the church's need to understand and connect with the community. This is what they call "breaking the missional code." They state, "Missionaries have known this for centuries. They know that they must have a profound understanding of their host culture before planning a strategy to reach the unique people group that exists in that cultural context. This is why they first study the culture to find strategies that will work among the people who live in that cultural setting. Missions history is filled with stories of great revivals because missionaries were able to 'break the code,' and the church exploded in their community. The missionaries found the redemptive window through which the gospel could shine" (Stetzer and Putman, *Breaking the Missional Code*, p. 2).

Large international companies recognize the same dynamic. A friend of mine has a granddaughter who works for a firm in Boston that trains American workers for overseas assignments. They teach these employees about the culture of the people with whom they will be interacting, working, and doing business.

Missional pastors who have gained a new appreciation and definition of their parish, are equipping their people in the same way and leading them to take a fresh look at their own changing community; working together as partners in the gospel, they are building new bridges across the rivers that separate them from their neighbors. As Stetzer and Putman write: "Breaking the missional code is a recognition that there are visible and invisible characteristics within a community that will make its people resistant to or responsive to the church and its gospel message. Discerning Christians discover those relevant issues and break through the resistance—so that the name and reality of Jesus Christ can be more widely known" (*Breaking the Missional Code*, p. 5).

Bridges come in different forms. I've crossed a creek on a fallen log. I've also been to Grandfather Mountain in western North Carolina, where there's a rope bridge that crosses over to another peak—with a bottomless pit below! It sways with the wind and foot traffic. It bounces. I couldn't cross it. I could barely walk across the Rio Grande Gorge Bridge, looking 650 feet down at the ribbon-like appearance of the Rio Grande. Scary!

Bridges are designed and built according to the landscape and the best engineering at the time. Some are simple and some are engineering marvels, yet they all serve one great function—connecting that which is divided physically, culturally, or spiritually from another. When the old bridges become unsafe or insufficient, new bridges are needed. This is where many churches are today. We as pastors must lead our churches to build new bridges, which will provide pathways to the perishing.

If it is an exaggeration to think of Charleston as the "holy" city, it's probably a stretch to think that your city, town, or community is holy as well. Perhaps there was a time when the church had that kind of influence in our communities and neighborhoods, when Christ-followers shone with the presence and power of God and salted the world through the character of their Spirit-filled lives. That's not so common today. And while the message of the cross is still the one bridge between a holy God and sinful man, we've got to figure out, and figure out soon, how to build new bridges to those who need to hear the message of the cross in such a way that they can understand it and embrace the one who died and rose again so that they might live.

"'Do you understand what you are reading?' Philip asked.
'How can I,' he said, 'unless someone explains it to me?'
So he invited Philip to come up and sit with him."

—ACTS 8:30B–31

# - CHAPTER ELEVEN -

# The Praying Priest

"Aim for perfection."

—2 CORINTHIANS 13:11

To be pickled in the solution of our twentieth-century church culture is to struggle in the new realities of twenty-first century. The jar we live in and the juice that saturates our souls distort and dilute our vision and understanding of who we are and whom we serve. This much is true: we are pickled priests who live in the midst of pickled people.

We stand at a critical juncture, not only in our personal lives, but also in the American church. We are at a multi-faceted, crucial crossroads where personal ministries and the mission of the church have converged simultaneously. This is no accident of history. This is the unfolding of a plan and purpose known by our Sovereign Lord before the first page of history was written with the dawning of light in the universe.

The solution is the problem, and the problem is the solution. Out of this crisis, a new movement of God is emerging as he brings judgment on his own family, cutting off and pruning the branches of his family tree. He is the Gardener. Peter put it this way: "For it is time for judgment to begin with the family of God; and if it begins with us, what will the outcome be for those who do not obey the gospel of God?" (1 Peter 4:17).

I somehow knew as a seminarian that the Lord had a lot of work to do in my life to prepare me and perfect me for the gospel ministry. So thirty-five years ago, I closed my "Pickled Priest" poem with these words: "Oh, gracious

Gawd. Make me a more perfect pickled priest." I realized at some level, even then, that I was pickled. I realize now just how much this has affected my life and ministry. I am coming to a new realization today that there is much in me that needs perfecting. God is still perfecting and refining my life through new challenges and frequent chastening.

I am learning a new appreciation for Paul's "thorn in the flesh."

> To keep me from becoming conceited because of these surpassingly great revelations, there was given me a thorn in my flesh, a messenger of Satan, to torment me. Three times I pleaded with the Lord to take it away from me. But he said to me, "My grace is sufficient for you, for my power is made perfect in weakness." Therefore, I will boast all the more gladly about my weaknesses, so that Christ's power may rest on me. That is why, for Christ's sake, I delight in weaknesses, in insults, in hardships, in persecutions, in difficulties. For when I am weak, then I am strong" (2 Cor. 12:7–10).

If, as we have said, revelation produces passion, it is pain that produces humility, and it is humility that induces the grace of God. And the grace of God reduces us to dependence on the Almighty, who then lifts us up in power for his glory in the church. True revival with God's people is always the manifestation of God's presence and power, conditioned by repentance, humility, and prayer. We are all familiar with the Lord's words to Solomon: "If my people, who are called by my name, will humble themselves and pray and seek my face and turn from their wicked ways, then I will hear from heaven and will forgive their sin and will heal their land" (2 Chron. 7:14).

Having heard these haunting but hopeful words so many times, we must move beyond familiarity with these words to faithfully following its precepts and promise. Then perhaps we will experience a time of refreshing and restoration like the people of Hezekiah's day.

Before Hezekiah was king, Ahaz reigned sixteen years in Jerusalem. It is difficult to comprehend everything the Scripture attributes to him. He made and worshiped idols and offered sacrifices to the gods of other nations. Because of this, the Lord handed him one crushing defeat after another. But the Scripture says, "In his time of trouble, King Ahaz became even more unfaithful to the Lord" (2 Chron. 28:22).

As if this was not enough, he shut down the Lord's house. He closed the temple doors and cut off the lights. "Ahaz gathered together the furnishings from the temple of God and took them away. He shut the doors of the Lord's temple and set up altars at every street corner in Jerusalem. In every town in Judah he built high places to burn sacrifices to other gods and provoked the Lord, the God of his fathers, to anger" (2 Chron. 28:24–25). Quite a record if you're looking to get on the List of the World's Lousiest Rulers! Thankfully, the old adage, "Like father, like son," didn't apply to Hezekiah, his son and heir to the throne. Perhaps as a tribute to his mother's influence, the Scripture says of Hezekiah, "His mother's name was Abijah daughter of Zechariah. He did what was right in the eyes of the Lord, just as his father David had done," which puts him in good company as a leader.

As presidents in this country attempt to take advantage of the positive momentum of their first one hundred days in office to push through certain legislation and policies, Hezekiah didn't waste any time in getting down to business. The first item of business on his agenda was to right some wrongs and reverse the damage his father had inflicted on the nation.

The Scripture says, "In the first month of the first year of his reign, he opened the doors of the temple of the Lord and repaired them" (2 Chron. 29:3). Following that significant action, he ordered the consecration of all the priests and Levites along with the consecration and cleansing of the temple. Then he issued a challenge to the priests. He said, "My sons, do not be negligent now, for the Lord has chosen you to stand before him and serve him, to minister before him and to burn incense" (2 Chron. 29:11).

Then in the second month of his reign, Hezekiah sent word throughout the country, imploring the people to come to Jerusalem for the celebration of the Passover. The chronicler explains that the Passover had been neglected for some time because not enough priests had not been consecrated and the people had stopped coming. Imagine that. As a result of Hezekiah's strong appeal, the chronicler indicates that "a very large crowd of people assembled in Jerusalem to celebrate the Feast of Unleavened Bread in the second month. They removed the altars in Jerusalem and cleared away the incense altars and threw them in the Kidron Valley" (2 Chron. 30:13).

These pilgrims from all over Judah, with a renewed zeal for the living God, cleaned house, so to speak, and took all of Ahaz's junk to the landfill.

This time of revival in Jerusalem was so powerful and refreshing that "the whole assembly" decided to extend it another week. So with great joy, they celebrated for seven more days. That's revival! Then we notice something about the priests in all this. The Scripture says, "There was great joy in Jerusalem, for since the days of Solomon son of David king of Israel there had been nothing like this in Jerusalem. The priests and the Levites stood to bless the people, and God heard them, for their prayer reached heaven, his holy dwelling place" (2 Chron. 30:26–27). Whether you like the term or not, we are priests of the living God. May we, therefore, so consecrate ourselves that we can stand before God and serve him for our people, and may our prayers be heard in heaven, the holy dwelling place of God.

We may live in an Ahaz kind of time, but a Hezekiah kind of time is coming, I believe. Leaders must emerge as Hezekiah kind of leaders— leaders who are bold, courageous, and swift-acting. The church must have leaders who will make it their first order of business to repair and reopen the doors of the church, allowing people to enter in for authentic, consecrated worship. But reopened doors will also be the doors through which we release people and send people into the mission field.

Hezekiah reminds us that as priests of God we stand before the people for God and stand before God for the people. We are mediators in this relationship and mediums of his revelation and message. I wholeheartedly believe in the doctrine of the priesthood of all believers. That is not in question. But I also believe we have a God-ordained call to the priesthood as pastors, and though our prayers are no more powerful than the prayers of others, our responsibility in prayer is greater. Our priestly service and prayers do matter.

In the postexilic restoration of Jerusalem, Nehemiah rightly receives a lot of credit for his leadership abilities; but Ezra, the priest, should not be forgotten in the renewal of spiritual life in Jerusalem. When Ezra arrived in Jerusalem, he was heartbroken to learn that so many of the men had married foreign women, contrary to what they knew was God's best for them as a nation. The Scripture then tells us that Ezra did what godly priests do in that situation. He went to the Lord in prayer in a very public way, not for show, but because he was the mediator between the people and the Lord. "While Ezra was praying and confessing, weeping and throwing himself down before the house of God, a large crowd of Israelites—men, women, and children—gathered around him. They too wept bitterly" (Ezra 10:1). Of course, all that drama might seem a little much for the Baptists among us! Nevertheless, the prayers of a priest do matter.

Figuratively, if not literally, church doors are being shut all across America. Who is shutting those doors is really inconsequential. What matters infinitely more is who will be courageous enough to reopen the doors; who will stand and serve; and who will pray for God's blessings on his people?

Our opportunity to make that difference we have always desired to make has come. Let us not pray for personal success or validation, but let us pray that in this hour for this time we will, as pickled priests, be made more perfect in our weaknesses, strengthened in his grace, and prepared to lead our people with vision and passion.

During the Passover celebration, Hezekiah did two things that are quite remarkable and worthy of note. First, he broke the rules; he threw caution to the wind and protocol out the window. Many of the people who had come to Jerusalem from the outlying areas of Judah had not undergone the purification procedures, "yet they ate the Passover, contrary to what was written"—that is, the rules and regulations of the law, the Passover protocol. But Hezekiah does something unheard of. He asks the Lord to give them a break! "But Hezekiah prayed for them, saying, 'May the Lord, who is good, pardon everyone who sets his heart on seeking God—the Lord, the God of his fathers—even if he is not clean according to the rules of the sanctuary.' And the Lord heard Hezekiah and healed the people." He heard and healed! Even though they weren't clean according to "church rules," they were seeking God with their hearts. I love what Hezekiah did there for the people.

I love what Hezekiah did for the priests as well. Here's the second notable thing he did: He encouraged the priests and Levites—the pastoral staff. The Scripture says he "spoke encouragingly" to them. We all know that a little encouragement goes a long way. It does in my life. I am so grateful that God has gifted people in the church and others in my life who practice the gift of encouragement. They always have a way of showing up right after the ones who have the gift of criticism! It helps. We all need a Hezekiah or a Barnabas in our lives, someone who will "speak encouragingly" to us, or someone who can say, "I understand," and you know that they do.

That has been my aim and prayer in the writing of this book: that somehow what I've shared here would arrive at the place where you are—perhaps in that lonely place at the back of the fridge that we know as church—like a surprise package from an old friend, and that it will "spur" you on "toward love and good deeds." You are not alone. There are many of us. So let us together aim for perfection and pray for one another as we pray for our people and our parish. We can be priests to one another. We can be prophets to our people. More than prisoners to our culture, we are prisoners of Christ in these days of crisis and hope for the church. The struggle for the souls of people—people who are perishing—is worth it. It is always worth it.

"Now to him who is able to do immeasurably more than all we ask or imagine, according to his power that is at work within us, to him be glory in the church and in Christ Jesus throughout all generations, for ever and ever. Amen."

—EPHESIANS 3:20–21

# CHAPTER TWELVE

# Bouncing Back

"Humble yourselves before the Lord,
and he will lift you up."

—JAMES 4:10

Imagine that you are staying at a large hotel, and late one night you wander by one of the big ballrooms. Out of curiosity, you step inside for a peek. You look around the expansive room and take notice of what you see. The party is over and the crowd is thinning. There are a few people standing about, saying their farewells amid the mess of what appears to have been a rather gala event. The floor is covered with confetti and multicolored streamers. The once neatly adorned and decorated tabletops are in disarray. Half-filled and empty cups, soiled plates, and crumpled napkins clutter the room. The band members are unplugging their amps and breaking down the stage. A duo of hotel employees enters through another door. They glance quickly at their chore, and with unemotional and deliberate resolve, they spring into action. You feel some empathy for them, but after a party, someone has to clean up the mess.

As you turn to leave, something light lands on your head and bounces slightly in slow motion off your shoulders. It is so subtle and soft that it doesn't startle you. It's one of the many party balloons that were suspended for a while from the ceiling, floating with a brilliant flair, but it is in the process of deflation, falling gently and fading ingloriously as all balloons eventually do, its purpose past.

There are many boomer pastors who might identify with that deflated balloon. To them, the party is over and their purpose is past. Deflated and defeated, they are falling gently and fading ingloriously in the waning years of ministry. It's difficult to bounce back from that kind of mindset. There is virtually no bounce in a deflated balloon. A basketball without the proper air pressure will not bounce either. Anyone who has played a little basketball will identify with the frustration of trying to bounce a basketball that is even a little deflated.

There are many reasons those in ministry become deflated. As with automobile tires, there are many road hazards that puncture our hearts and minds and deflate our spirits. We go flat and sometimes experience a blowout. I sense that many boomer pastors today are sitting in their cars on the side of the freeway with a flat. Automobiles are screaming down the highway, night is falling, it's beginning to rain, and they sadly realize that they forgot to put the spare back in the trunk the day before. It might be a hassle, but fixing a flat is much easier than fixing a punctured heart and a deflated spirit.

This may seem a bit exaggerated, and it probably is. The point is, there is a problem of deflation among boomer pastors, and we've got to get our bounce back! The Lord isn't through with us, and if it seems to us that the party is over, well, let's get on with starting a new party—a celebration of Christ's restoring work in us for the renewing of our ministries for the sake of the church and the kingdom.

To fix a flat, you plug the hole and fill the tire. To fix deflation requires inflation. The good news is that the Lord we serve specializes in inflation—the infilling of his love, life, and power in the inner man—especially when we're stranded, helpless, and desperate for his help and healing. This filling, of course, is for all God's people.

As Paul suffered for the cause of Christ, he wrote to the church at Ephesus from his prison cell in Rome. He admonished them not to be discouraged about his suffering for their sake. This was his prayer for them in Ephesians 3:14–21: "For this reason I kneel before the Father from whom his whole family in heaven and on earth derives its name. I pray that out of his glorious riches he may strengthen you with power through his Spirit in your inner being, so that Christ may dwell in your hearts through faith. And I pray that you, being rooted and established in love, may have power, together with all the saints, to grasp how wide and long and high and deep is the love of Christ, and to know this love that surpasses knowledge—that you may be filled to the measure of all the fullness of God. Now to him who is able to do immeasurably more than all we ask or imagine, according to his power that is at work within us, to him be glory in the church and in Christ Jesus throughout all generations, for ever and ever! Amen."

That is the kind of prayer I pray for all of us who are deflated servants of the Lord Jesus Christ. I pray that we will once again be inflated with the love and power of Christ in our inner being—"filled to the measure of the fullness of God,"—that God will be glorified through our lives and in our churches. This filling is the promise of God in every generation, even in our generation as boomers and in this challenging time in which we serve.

Deflated spiritual leaders can bounce back when they seek this filling. Paul later exhorted the church at Ephesus, "Be very careful, then, how you live—not as unwise but as wise, making the most of every opportunity, because the days are evil. Therefore do not be foolish, but understand what the Lord's will is. Do not get drunk on wine, which leads to debauchery. Instead, be filled with the Spirit" (Eph. 5:15–18).

I doubt that many of us are dealing with a drinking problem. It's probably been a long time since we were *pickled* in the sense of alcoholic intoxication, if ever. But as pickled priests, we may have filled our lives in the recent past with the intoxicating effects of other worldly attitudes and things that keep us from experiencing the full effects and fruit of the Spirit's fullness in our lives. As boomers, we are prone to be pickled by fleshly power, position, and popularity. This eventually leads to deflation. Like a party balloon, there is a shelf life to self-inflation.

Henri Nouwen wrote a magnificent book entitled *In the Name of Jesus: Reflections on Christian Leadership* in which I discovered an invaluable perspective on spiritual leadership. This small volume is filled with meaning for me. He writes about his own life experience of rising to professional prominence as a scholar and author. He had been on the faculty at Notre Dame, Yale, and Harvard and had authored several widely read books. Then came an unexpected turn in his professional life that taught him a whole new perspective on Christian leadership. He was asked to leave his prestigious position at Harvard and serve as a priest with the mentally handicapped at the L'Arche communities in Toronto.

With humility and honesty, he writes in the book's introduction: "After twenty-five years in the priesthood, I found myself praying poorly, living somewhat isolated from other people, and very much preoccupied with burning issues. Everyone was saying that I was doing really well, but something inside was telling me that my success was putting my soul in danger. I began to ask myself whether my lack of contemplative prayer, my loneliness, and my constantly changing involvement in what seemed most urgent were signs that the Spirit was gradually being suppressed. It was very hard for me to see clearly, and though I never spoke about hell or jokingly so, I woke up one day with the realization that I was living in a very dark place and that term "burnout" was a convenient psychological translation for a spiritual death" (Henri Nouwen, *In the Name of Jesus: Reflections on Christian Leadership*, pp. 10–11).

Nouwen's ministry among the residents at the L'Arche gave him new insight into the Scriptures, a renewed fellowship with Jesus, and a deeper understanding of what it means to be the kind of leader that is first led by Jesus himself. Drawing on Jesus' three temptations in the desert, Nouwen suggests that the leaders of the twenty-first century must be careful not to fall victim to these same temptations: to be relevant, to be spectacular (popular), and to be powerful. With all three temptations, Nouwen takes us to the account in John 20 where Jesus challenges Peter about his love for the Lord and his call to be a shepherd of the sheep. "Simon, Son of John, do you truly love me more than these? Feed my sheep."

Christian leaders today need to answer that exact question and fulfill that same command. Nouwen writes: "Here we touch the most important quality of Christian leadership for the future. It is not a leadership of power and control, but a leadership of powerlessness and humility in which the suffering servant of God, Jesus Christ, is made manifest. I, obviously, am not speaking about a psychologically weak leadership in which the Christian leader is simply the passive victim of the manipulations of his milieu. No, I am speaking of a leadership in which power is constantly abandoned in favor of love. It is a true spiritual leadership. Powerlessness and humility in the spiritual life do not refer to people who have no spine and who let everyone else make decisions for them. They refer to people who are so deeply in love with Jesus that they are ready to follow him wherever he guides them, always trusting that, with him, they will find life and find it abundantly" (Nouwen, pp. 63–64).

Could it be that our deflation is less a result of road hazards—wounds inflicted by the outside world—and more from the inner condition of a heart that is loveless when it comes to our own personal relationship with Christ, replaced by a love for fleshly things? In having lost that first love somewhere along the way, have we not lost the abundant life we eagerly urge upon others?

The word *abundant* means "exceedingly full." The abundant life Jesus came to give us is a life that is exceedingly full of the life and love of Jesus, a life that lives for Jesus and loves him exceedingly. According to Paul, that is what it means to be filled with the Spirit. The Spirit is the Spirit of Christ, which is the Spirit of life, power, and truth. The temptations of leadership are to pursue counterfeit values that mimic the true values we find only when we are devoid and deflated of self.

As boomers, it is in our generational character to be idealistic, competitive, and achievement-driven, which makes us especially vulnerable to the desert temptations of relevance, popularity, and power. Many of us have taken the bait dangled out there by the evil one, and we are only now realizing how empty and dissatisfied we really are. Yet, if we are wise to our dilemma and to our time, we have an incredible opportunity to be filled with the Spirit. That's how we can bounce back!

Other leaders have made great comebacks in their time. David was one of those leaders who bounced back many times. He bounced back when others thought he was down for the count. He bounced back from many adversities and from his own personal failures. He wrote Psalm 63 while in a desert place. He was hungry, thirsty, desperate, and deflated, and in his desperation he sought the Lord. "O God, you are my God, earnestly I seek you; my soul thirsts for you, my body longs for you, in a dry and weary land where there is no water. I have seen you in the sanctuary and beheld your power and your glory. Because your love is better than life, my lips will glorify you. I will praise you as long as I live, and in your name I will lift up my hands. My soul will be satisfied as with the richest of foods; with singing lips my mouth will praise you" (Ps. 63:1–5).

This was the prayer of a bounced-back man of God, a leader who believed that the love of God was better than life. He was down, but he wasn't out. He believed that in seeking to reconnect in a deeply personal way with God, his soul would be satisfied, exceedingly filled with the bread and breath of heaven.

The Scripture says it is pride that precedes a fall. The way back up is the way of humility. Pride puffs us up and inflates us with self-importance and self-sufficiency. Pride, however, is a heavy gas, like carbon monoxide, and we suffocate in it. With pride, we gloat but never float. We sink and fall. Humility, like helium, is a light gas, and ironically we are brought low when we are filled with it. As we humble ourselves and lose all sense of self-importance and self-sufficiency, it is the Lord who lifts us up. It is the paradox of the cross. In losing our lives in Christ, we find it again, along with a new way of understanding our calling and a quality of leadership that is empowered by the inflation—the filling—of the Holy Spirit in the inner man.

The outer circumstances of changing culture, our current parish, and our own personal challenges, inform our calling, but these are conditional and contextual matters. What matters is the inner man. Do we truly love Jesus? Do we truly love him more than "these"? If our answer is a thoughtful, heartfelt "Yes!" then we feed the sheep, leading them through the dark valleys into the green pastures. When we lead our sheep fearlessly through the dark valleys, we get to a better place ourselves.

It is good to remember that even as pastors, we have a Good Shepherd who has laid down his life for us. By his hand, we will never be in want. He will guide us down righteous paths. He will lead us beside still waters, anoint our heads with oil, and restore our souls. He will fill our cups exceedingly—to running over—with goodness and mercy.

All men fall into the sin of pride, not the least of which are servants of God. There is a significant difference between prideful leaders who fall but never recover and those who do. Some leaders would rather die than confess that they have a problem with pride. That was the difference between Saul and David.

Saul and David both received the anointing of God, but Saul became increasingly prideful and controlled by the sinful nature. While Saul was still reigning as God's anointed, David increasingly gained the favor of God and the people. "Saul has slain his thousands, and David his tens of thousands" (1 Sam. 18:7). Saul's pride manifested in great jealousy, his jealousy became dangerous and destructive, and in the end, he fell on his own sword.

In contrast, consider how David dealt with personal failure. In 1 Chronicles 21, we read about a time of spiritual weakness when David succumbed to pride as Satan tempted him in the taking of a census. Taking a census in and of itself wasn't a sin, but it was David's motivation that was the problem. It was not a counting of the people that was wrong so much as David's intent on counting the fighting men in Israel to bolster his sense of power and authority. He lost sight of the blessings of God and began to see himself in a prideful way. "Look at me. Look at what I have accomplished and all that I command."

As soon as the census was over, David became convicted of his sin. "Then David said to God, 'I have sinned greatly by doing this. Now, I beg you, take away the guilt of your servant. I have done a very foolish thing'" (1 Chron. 21:8). What happened after that reminds us that sin always carries a consequence. God is faithful and just to forgive us, but the consequences remain. Furthermore, those with close connections to us feel these consequences. The larger one's sphere of influence, the greater the number of people who will be affected by one's sin. The sins of a father may only affect his family. The sins of a church leader may affect hundreds. The sins of a CEO of a large corporation may affect thousands. The sins of a national leader may affect millions.

David's pride brought incredible suffering on his people. Seventy-five thousand men died in a God-sent plague. The Scripture doesn't tell us how many women and children died. David was broken, his pride all gone. He cried out to God, "Was it not I who ordered the fighting men to be counted? I am the one who has sinned and done wrong. These are but sheep. What have they done? O Lord my God, let your hand fall upon me and my family, but do not let this plague remain on your people" (1 Chron. 21:17). In response, God instructed David to build an altar to the Lord on the threshing floor of a man named Araunah, which he did, offering burnt offerings and fellowship offerings in humble, heartfelt worship on his knees before the Lord.

The difference between Saul and David is stark and profound. When Saul, filled with pride, realized his failure as a leader, he fell on his own sword. When David realized his own pride and the consequences it brought upon his people, he fell on his knees. One lost his life and his kingdom. The other was promised a kingdom that would never end.

There is one more thought about Saul and David that relates to boomer pastors. Saul saw David as a threat, but David was a threat only to the extent that Saul was forfeiting his integrity as a servant of God. The anointing was his until by his own arrogance he dishonored it. David's integrity of character is nowhere more evident than his refusal to harm Saul, though he had opportunity to do so. On at least two occasions, he spared Saul's life, saying, "I will not lay a hand on the Lord's anointed." David understood God's calling and promise on his life, but he was willing to wait until the proper time to exercise that calling and promise.

As boomer pastors, we are well aware that there are some young David's nipping at our heels, if not nipping at our reputations. These young men are full of youthful ambition, admirable passion, and enormous talent that God will certainly use if they carefully guard their hearts and keep their integrity. I would urge my fellow boomer pastors to guard their hearts against Saul-like jealousy and resentment. I would likewise urge these young David's to demonstrate a little respect for their older brothers. I would caution them against prideful ambition and urge them to learn humility, to exercise restraint, and to practice patience.

Know this: we boomer pastors will go, but we will not go the way of Saul. We will not fall on our swords. We will fall on our knees and cry, "Oh, God, make me a more perfect pickled priest!"

> "Search me, O God, and know my heart; test me and
> know my anxious thoughts. See if there is any offensive
> way in me, and lead me in the way everlasting."

—PSALM 139:23–24

CPSIA information can be obtained at www.ICGtesting.com
Printed in the USA
237476LV00002B/5/P

9 781615 079155